The STARS and STRIPES

The Stars and Stripes: Fabric of the American Spirit
is published by J. Richard Pierce, LLC

First Edition July 2005

ISBN: 0-9769469-0

Editor: Sarah Novak
Photography: Michael Fredericks
Design: Ron Toelke, Toelke Associates
Special thanks to Jeffrey Kenneth Kohn, M.D.

Printed in the U.S.A.

*This flag, which we honor and under which we serve,
is the emblem of our unity, our power, our thought and purpose
as a nation. It has no other character than that which we give it
from generation to generation.... And yet, though silent, it speaks
to us—speaks to us of the past, of the men and women who
went before us, and all of the records they wrote upon it.*

President Woodrow Wilson
Flag Day, 1917

The
STARS *and*
STRIPES
Fabric *of* the American Spirit

J. Richard Pierce

The Pierce Collection of American Parade Flags

Dedicated to the brave men and women who sacrificed so much to protect our freedoms and preserve our way of life.

CONTENTS

FOREWORD

As a psychiatrist, I frequently dealt with various aspects of the human condition, from passions to phobias. Paralleling my career as an antiques dealer, I have interacted with a unique group of individuals called "collectors." All true collectors have a passion that can rarely be understood by mere mortals.

As with all collectors, Richard started with interest in an object common to his life experience but only superficially explored: the American flag. His wife, Barbara, purchased a vintage flag as a surprise thirtieth wedding anniversary gift for Richard. A fire was then lit. Shortly thereafter, Richard met me at an antiques show. I was beginning to exhibit and sell mounted flags that offered a combination of great graphics, an unusual folk art quality to their design, and a historical connection. Richard purchased first one, then a couple more, then many more flags. I had little warning that such zeal was inflamed, and that it would motivate Richard to secure, for his ever-growing collection, the best, often unique examples, of American parade flags whenever they come into the marketplace.

The real zeal of his collecting only gradually revealed itself. Richard was not just collecting the flags but also the long-forgotten thoughts, feelings, and memories that were woven into the fabric of each flag he added to his collection. Each flag, with no remaining voice, became a reminder why it was used and preserved. One can only imagine the passion and drive that pushed Richard to decipher the names, initials, and messages written on these parade flags.

I can readily imagine the smile on a young woman's face when she returned from the dance and wrote "SOUVENIOR OF ST. MARY'S JUNIOR DANCE JAN 29, 1938" on the stick of her forty-eight-star flag. I still get goose bumps when I look at that thirty-five-star parade flag that Florence G.S. waved from her porch that "Lincoln's men saluted" as they sang "Rally Round the Flag Boys" marching in their torchlight parade off to war. I can only imagine who will be the future collectors of the flags that many of us hang from our cars, homes, and businesses in response to the tragedy of 9/11, and only now putting them into drawers, trunks, and attics. I am confident that these flags will be preserved because the flame that ignited Richard into forming this collection to honor and cherish our flag has become a torch that will be passed on to future generations.

Jeffrey Kenneth Kohn, M.D.
Flag Day 2005

INTRODUCTION

For as long as I can remember, the American flag has held special meaning for me. Perhaps it was my lifelong interest in politics or my appreciation for the freedoms the flag represents that first enticed me to learn more about its history and later to begin collecting. Whatever the reasons, it is a passion.

To me, the flag is the symbol of our individual freedoms, traditions, and national unity, as well as an enduring memorial to the men and women who sacrificed so much to preserve our way of life. It is a lasting tribute to the founding fathers of our great republic and their foresight and wisdom in framing the Constitution and the Bill of Rights. For more than two centuries, the flag has been America's most revered and sacred national emblem and, for generation after generation, has occupied a special place in the hearts of all Americans.

This collection of American parade flags is more than just an assemblage of the Stars and Stripes: it is a repository for the many memories that might otherwise have been forgotten or lost in history. In my view, preserving the thoughts and precious moments that someone recorded on paper or on the flag itself is equally as important as acquiring flags with rare or unique star pattern designs. It is essential that these moments in time, some dating back nearly one hundred and fifty years, be cared for and passed on for the benefit of those who follow after us.

Parade flags were most often printed to wave at a special celebration, parade, holiday event or political rally, and then discarded. They were not made for use over an extended period of time, which explains why so many have not survived through the years.

As I look at the flags hanging on the walls of my study and throughout our home, I sense and appreciate the history each represents. Many are handmade, and I wonder who took strips of red and white cotton or silk, cut out individual white stars, and meticulously sewed them together to create a flag. Was it sewn for a soldier going off to war or made to be waved at a holiday parade or special celebration? An important part of my overall collecting enjoyment is researching each flag to learn about its origin in hopes of finding the answers to these and other questions.

When I think about some of the most dramatic moments in our history—Washington crossing the Delaware, Francis Scott Key seeing that tattered flag flying over Fort McHenry and being inspired to write "The Star-Spangled Banner," the marines raising the flag on Iwo Jima, and recently, the three firefighters hoisting the flag on a steel beam at the ruins of the World Trade Center—the one common symbol that embodies the greatness of each of these moments and epitomizes the true American spirit is the American flag.

The evolution of the Stars and Stripes reflects the growth of the nation and dates back to June 14, 1777, when the Continental Congress adopted a resolution creating the first official flag. "Resolved, that the flag of the United States be made of thirteen stripes, alternate red and white, that the union be thirteen stars, white on a blue field, representing a new constellation." No one knows for certain who sewed the first flag, but historians credit the design to Francis Hopkinson, a delegate to the Continental Congress from New Jersey, chairman of the Continental navy board and one of the signers of the Declaration of Independence.

In 1795, following the admission of Vermont and Kentucky as the fourteenth and fifteenth states, Congress authorized a second official flag with fifteen stars and fifteen stripes. Although additional states joined the union in the years following, the fifteen-star flag remained the official flag until 1818 when Mississippi was admitted as the twentieth state.

Realizing the nation would continue to grow but adding a new star and stripe for each new state was not a practical approach, New York congressman Peter Wendover requested Captain Samuel Reid of the U.S. Navy to develop a flag design that would replace the fifteen-star flag and allow for adding new states while retaining the overall distinctive character of the flag. Reid recommended a basic flag design of thirteen alternate red and white stripes honoring the original thirteen colonies, and a star for each state, with a new star added on July 4 following admission of each new state to the union. Congress incorporated these recommendations into the Second Flag Act of 1818; however, Reid's recommendation to configure the stars into a

Great Star pattern was not included, nor was any standard specified in the final legislation for the placement of stars. For nearly the next one hundred years, the pattern of stars representing the states was left to the discretion of the flag maker.

During the nation's centennial celebration in 1876, the popularity of the flag greatly increased, and reproductions of earlier flag designs and handmade, one-of-a-kind examples were created. Although variations of the wreath pattern were most popular, flag makers produced a variety of imaginative and unusual star configurations, including double medallions, Great Star, diamond, pentagon, global, and square designs, as well as various combinations thereof.

In 1912, the star pattern and dimensions of the forty-eight-star flag were established by executive order of President Taft, based on recommendations of a joint board of army and navy officers with Admiral George Dewey serving as its senior member. This flag, commemorating Arizona statehood, was official for forty-seven years, longer than any other flag to date, and is associated with eight presidents, two World Wars, and many other momentous events in United States history. The fifty-star flag honored today is the twenty-seventh official flag and will soon become the longest-lived in American history.

Since its humble beginning in 1777, the flag has remained the most sacred national icon of the United States, the definitive symbol of this great republic. It traces the country's past and represents the principles of freedom and equality that are the foundation of the nation. The flag is the symbol of what the people of America stand for, what we believe in, and what defines us as citizens of the greatest country in the history of the world. It is the spirit of our individual hopes and dreams, and the shining light for democracy everywhere.

The Stars and Stripes rallies Americans in times of celebration as well as giving us the strength we need to carry on during times of peril. The flag is the symbol of our very foundation; it is the fabric that binds us together . . . it is the fabric of the American spirit.

J. Richard Pierce

A New Constellation

The Continental Congress adopted the Flag Act creating America's first official flag on June 14, 1777, a year after the signing of the Declaration of Independence. The resolution specified the flag to have thirteen red and white stripes, and thirteen white stars on a blue field representing a new constellation.

Until 1912, no regulation governed the arrangement or uniformity of the stars; as a result, flag makers used a variety of graphic design elements such as various sized stars, haloed stars, upside down stars, and stars tilted in different directions. Also, there are many examples of notched and staggered patterns and others that left space for additional stars to be incorporated into the design. At the same time, newly developed printing techniques were being introduced in the manufacturing process that produced flags.

The United States expanded rapidly during the second half of the nineteenth century as new states joined the union. For this reason, it was not uncommon for the American people to continue using flags with fewer than the official number of stars.

Hand-sewn cotton and appliquéd four-pointed stars. Canton extends full width of flag with stars configured randomly in upper left corner. Twelve stripes in white and red sequence.

This rare flag was made in Maine for Ossian Preston Ingraham when he was a young boy. Born in Kenduskeag, Maine, in 1847, Ossian and his parents Joseph and Nancy (Cole) Ingraham lived there until moving to California in 1863. He was initiated into Kenduskeag Division No. 225 Sons of Temperance, an organization established to shield its members from the evils of intemperance, to offer mutual assistance in times of sickness, and to reclaim those who fell under the influence of strong drink.

Among the documents accompanying this flag is a letter written by Ossian to his daughter Eleanor on April 27, 1906, nine days after the great San Francisco earthquake, in which he describes the devastation and living conditions in the aftermath of that horrible tragedy.

Flag size: 25" x 12"

15-STAR FLAG • Ca. 1876–92

Printed on glazed cotton muslin. Wreath pattern with central star, flanked by star in each corner.

After the French and Indian Wars, settlers began moving westward into the Kentucky territory. James Harrod and his surveying party established Harrodsburg, the first settlement, in 1774; the Commonwealth of Kentucky was admitted to the union as the fifteenth state in 1792, the first west of the Appalachians.

Most likely, this flag was produced during the centennial celebration in honor of Kentucky statehood.

Flag size: 8" x 5¼"

13-STAR FLAG • Ca. 1890

Printed on cotton. Naval ensign pattern. Fourteen stripes with broad red bar printed on left side of canton. Made in Canada for a special celebration.

This thirteen-star pattern was adopted by the U.S. Navy as its standard ensign for ships from the 1870s until 1916, when President Wilson issued an executive order officially discontinuing the customary use of thirteen-star flags on Navy vessels.

Flag size: 24" x 13"

Hand-sewn silk stripes and embroidered stars. Outer square pattern surrounding small wreath with central star.

The twenty-four-star flag is associated with the origin of one of our flag's most beloved nicknames. In 1831, on his twenty-first birth-day, Captain William Driver from Salem, Massachusetts, was given a handmade twenty-four-star flag which he named "Old Glory." He took the flag aboard his ship *Charles Doggett* and sailed twice around the world. Driver retired from the sea in 1837 and moved to Nashville where he proudly flew his flag. When Tennessee seceded from the Union, he was forced to hide it, but after Union soldiers recaptured Nashville, Driver climbed the state capitol tower and raised the flag. In 1922, his daughter passed "Old Glory" on to President Warren G. Harding who in turn presented it to the Smithsonian Institution.

Flag size: 9" x 6"

Printed on cotton; commemorates Michigan statehood. Double medallion pattern with central star, flanked by star in each corner.

The completion of the Erie Canal in 1825 enabled settlers from eastern states to migrate to the Michigan Territory more easily, and within ten years there was sufficient population to apply for statehood. Following the resolution of a boundary dispute with Ohio over an area that is now the city of Toledo, Michigan became the twenty-sixth state on January 26, 1837.

Parade flags made before the Civil War are extremely rare, and less than a dozen twenty-six-star flags are known to exist, most of which are Great Star patterns. This double medallion with various-sized stars is unique in its design and may be one of the few surviving examples.

Flag size: 27½" x 21"

Printed on homespun cotton. Great Star pattern.

At the request of a congressional committee in 1818, naval hero Captain Samuel Reid recommended a new design to replace the existing flag of fifteen stars and fifteen stripes. Rather than adding an additional stripe and star for each new state, Reid suggested standardizing the use of thirteen stripes, representing the original colonies, and configuring the stars, one for each state, into a Great Star pattern, with stars for newly admitted states added on July 4 following the year of statehood. The Third Flag Act signed by President Monroe specified thirteen stripes, alternating red and white, and a star for each state; however, the arrangement of the stars was not defined in the final legislation enacted by Congress.

Great Star patterns were most commonly used until the end of the nineteenth century.

Flag size: 28" x 21"

29-STAR FLAG • Ca. 1847–48

Printed on glazed cotton muslin; commemorates Iowa statehood. Double medallion pattern with central star, flanked by star in each corner.

During the presidency of James Polk, expansionists believed it was America's manifest destiny to extend its borders westward to the Pacific, and it was during the period 1845-49 that the United States acquired its largest territorial gains.

The admission of five states in six years made it difficult for flag makers to keep abreast of new star requirements, and most likely the average American commonly displayed a flag with fewer than the official number of stars.

Flag size: 10" x 7"

30-STAR FLAG • Ca. 1848–51

Paint-printed on cotton; commemorates Wisconsin statehood.

Wisconsin was designated a territory in 1836 and during the next few years the region's population grew rapidly from an influx of German, Irish, and Scandinavian immigrants. The rich soil and agricultural potential also attracted a considerable number of easterners who arrived via the Erie Canal and Great Lakes. After rejecting statehood propositions four times, the citizens of Wisconsin voted to become a state in May 1848.

Flag size: 27" x 20"

31-STAR GREAT STAR FLAG
Ca. 1851–58

Printed on glazed cotton muslin; commemorates California statehood. Great Star pattern with outlying star between each point.

The Great Star pattern has an extraordinary folk art quality and is widely regarded as the most beautiful of the Stars and Stripes. This magnificent configuration in an unusual offset pattern was likely transformed from an earlier twenty-six-star design.

Flag size: 32" x 24"

34-STAR FLAG • Ca. 1861–63

Printed on cotton; commemorates Kansas statehood. Double medallion pattern with large central star, flanked by a star in each corner and one outlying star.

The thirty-four-star flag became official on July 4, 1861, several months after South Carolina, Alabama, Florida, Georgia, Louisiana, Mississippi, and Texas seceded from the union and formed the Confederate States of America in February, 1861. Two months later, Confederate troops attacked and captured Fort Sumter, marking the beginning of the Civil War.

Flag size: 22" x 14"

Printed on silk. Transition between Great Star and pentagon patterns.

Known as Lincoln's flag, the thirty-four-star flag became official several months after the secession of seven southern states from the Union; President Lincoln refused to allow the elimination of any stars when the new flag was created.

On the way to his inauguration in February 1861, President-elect Lincoln attended a ceremony in Philadelphia honoring the birthday of George Washington. He used the occasion to raise a thirty-four-star flag over Independence Hall in a courageous act of faith and a bold gesture of national unity.

Flag size: 13½" x 9¾"

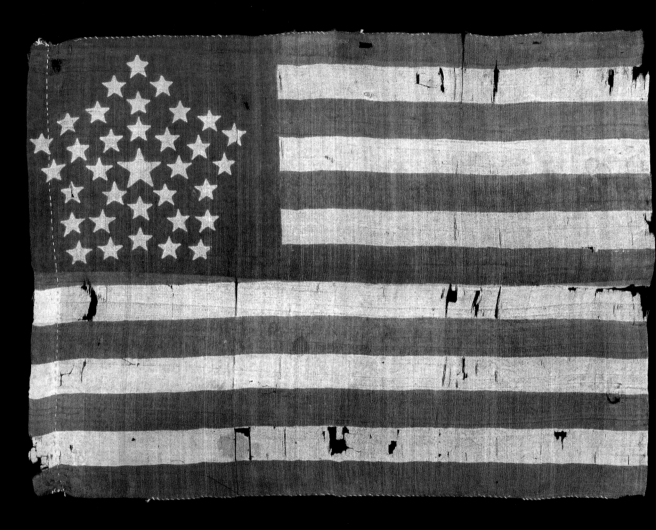

34-STAR GREAT STAR FLAG • Ca. 1861–63

Printed on cotton. Great Star pattern.

The thirty-four stars form a perfect pentagram, unlike earlier flower-like Great Star patterns. One of similar design, edged with a band of black crepe, was used as a mourning flag for Abraham Lincoln and other assassinated presidents.

Flag size: 40" x 24½"

36-STAR FLAG • Ca. 1865–67

Printed on glazed cotton muslin; commemorates Nevada statehood. Bracketed wreath pattern, with central star, flanked by star in each corner.

Nevada was created as a federal territory in 1861 in an effort to ensure that its gold and silver resources would be used to help the Union cause and not the Confederacy. After the Civil War ended, the Thirteenth Amendment, abolishing slavery, was enacted by Congress and sent to the states for ratification. The search for a sufficient number of states to pass the amendment led to the acceleration of statehood for Nevada, which was admitted in October 1864, even though it lacked sufficient population under normal rules for statehood.

Flag size: 13¾" x 8"

41-STAR FLAG • Ca. 1889

Printed on cotton; commemorates Montana statehood. Staggered pattern. Rare star count.

On November 2, 1889, North Dakota and South Dakota were added as the thirty-ninth and fortieth states, the first time in history two states were admitted on the same day. Montana became the forty-first state on November 8, predating Washington, the forty-second state, by three days. As a result of these rapid changes in the number of states, only a very small number of forty-one-star flags was ever produced, thereby making it extremely rare.

Flag size: 24½" x 15½"

42-STAR HALO FLAG • Ca. 1889–90

Paint-printed on cotton. Double medallion pattern with haloed central star, flanked by three stars in each corner.

This flag, commemorating Washington statehood, incorporates the latest known use of the halo star design, which originated during the Civil War period. The central star represents the state of Washington which joined the union in November 1899, one of four states to gain statehood that year.

Flag size: 13" x 8"

45-STAR FLAG • Ca. 1896–1908

Machine-sewn silk stripes; commemorates Utah statehood. Embroidered stars in seldom-used pattern of five rows of nine stars.

The Territory of Utah was included in the vast land domain acquired by the United States under terms of the Treaty of Guadalupe-Hidalgo signed at the end of the Mexican War in 1848. From the time of annexation, the federal government and the Mormon political leadership disputed the Mormon custom of polygamy. Utah eventually banned the practice and was admitted as the forty-fifth state in January 1896.

The attached cotton cord was used to tie the flag together with a group of international flags to form a celebration banner.

Flag size: 12" x 8½"

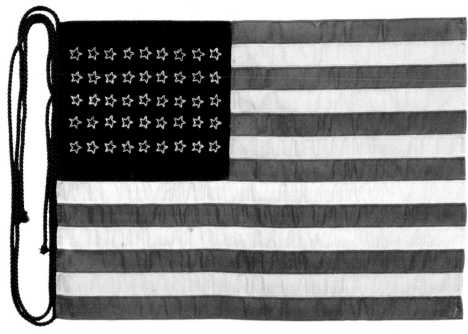

47-STAR FLAG • Ca. 1912

Printed on silk; commemorates New Mexico statehood. Rare star count.

Admitted to the union on January 6, 1912, New Mexico had taken more than fifty years to gain statehood, initially granted territorial status by Congress through the Compromise of 1850. Several attempts to pass a state constitution were defeated; many in Congress were concerned about the inhabitants' race and religion, as well as economic considerations.

New Mexico was followed shortly thereafter by Arizona statehood on February 14, making the forty-seven-star flag the unofficial flag of the United States for thirty-nine days.

Flag size: 12" x 7"

Centennial Celebration

The occasion of the nation's one hundredth birthday inspired a renewed patriotism that swept across America. Large cities and small towns alike hosted parades; throughout the nation, public buildings, businesses, and homes were decorated with flags and red, white, and blue banners.

The centennial was a period of national celebration, with the flag as the primary symbol of American idealism and national pride. It was a time when flag designers, limited only by their own imagination, created flags with a variety of different star patterns. Several flag variations, some with words printed across the stripes, were designed as a tribute to the nation's progress and to commemorate the first one hundred years of American history.

The Civil War had ended a decade earlier, and Americans were once again beginning to come together. The centennial provided the perfect opportunity not only to celebrate a century of progress but to look ahead with vision and hope for the future as one country, one people.

Printed on wool and cotton blend. Stars are embellished with a thin line between each point to create a glimmering effect and are configured to form the years "1776" (composed of thirty-eight stars) and "1876."

A masterpiece in design, this is one of several commemorative flags specially produced for America's centennial celebration.

Flag size: 39" x 28"

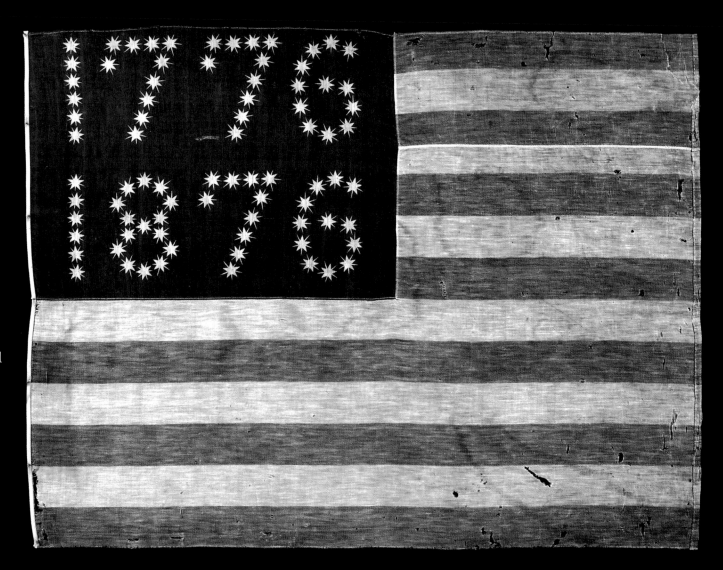

36-STAR CENTENNIAL EXHIBITION FLAG • Ca. 1876

Silk exhibition flag. Staggered pattern. Inscriptions read:

[Obverse] *Philadelphia International Exhibition*
America and France Union Forever
1776 Centennial 1876 Souvenir
[Reverse] *Philadelphia International Exhibition*
Union For Ever 1776 Centennial 1876 Memento

The Centennial Exhibition, celebrating one hundred years of American cultural and industrial progress, was held at the Fairmount Park fairgrounds in Philadelphia and marked the first time a major world's fair was held in the United States. The event was immensely popular and introduced America as a new industrial world power.

Although there were thirty-seven states when the exhibition opened, this souvenir flag was produced with thirty-six stars, illustrating the liberty sometimes taken by flag makers to favor graphic design over historical accuracy.

Flag size: 4¾" x 2¾"

38-STAR CENTENNIAL FLAG • Ca. 1876

Printed on cotton. Rare example of printed gold stars.
Inscription in selvage reads:

Philadelphia, Sept 1876, G.N.M.

Printing reads:

Centennial 1876

Designed for the nation's centennial celebration, which opened in Philadelphia on May 10, 1876, this flag is unique for several reasons. The printing on the stripes is not an overprint but rather was incorporated when the flag was manufactured. Also, the use of gold stars on parade flags is virtually unknown. The canton was intentionally printed in the upper right corner.

Flag size: 24" x 16"

Hand-sewn cotton and appliquéd stars. Wreath pattern with central star, flanked by star in each corner.

After the Civil War and during the centennial celebration in 1876, a renewed patriotism inspired an increased respect for the Stars and Stripes and widespread display. Throughout the nation, homes, public buildings, and businesses were proudly decorated with flags and patriotic banners. Flag makers created a variety of configurations and among the most popular was a wreath pattern surrounding a large central star with a star in each corner.

Flag size: 29" x 19"

13-STAR CENTENNIAL FLAG • Ca. 1876

Machine-sewn cotton and hand-sewn appliqué stars. Wreath pattern with three stars in center forming a triangle.

   The popularity of the flag reached new heights after the Civil War, and Americans continued their love affair with the Stars and Stripes through the nation's one hundredth birthday celebration in 1876. One-of-a-kind flag designs epitomized the expression of individual freedom and a renewed faith in the founding principles of the republic.

   This flag is one of a few known examples in which the stars are configured in a wreath pattern surrounding a triangle of stars.

Flag size: 20" x 13"

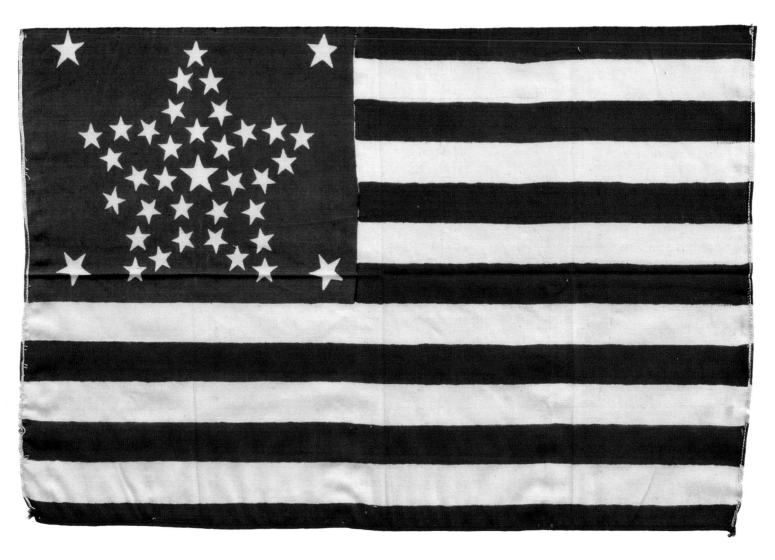

Printed on silk. Great Star pattern, flanked by star in each corner with one outlying star.

    This flag displays a beautiful and delicate design more like a great flower than a Great Star. First appearing on flags in 1818, this starry pattern was in use for a longer period of time than any other form of the Stars and Stripes.

Flag size: 17½" x 11½"

38-STAR FLAG • Ca. 1876–90

Printed on glazed cotton muslin. Global pattern with central star and one star in upper left and lower left corners.

The occasion of the nation's centennial provided American flag makers with a unique opportunity to create unusual and imaginative flag designs. Perhaps the globe-like design symbolized America's emergence as a world power and its far-reaching presence around the world.

Flag size: 12½" x 8¾"

GRAND UNION FLAG • Ca. 1876

Printed on wool.

The Continental Army was reorganized on January 1, 1776, under the command of General George Washington. On that day, Washington ordered the hoisting of the Grand Union flag above his camp at Prospect Hill, just outside of Boston, as a tribute to the united colonies.

Also known as the "Continental Colors," the flag featured joined crosses of St. George and St. Andrew in the canton. The Grand Union flag, predecessor to the Stars and Stripes, was flown on several ships during the period 1776–77 and was the first American flag to be recognized by another country.

Flag size: 35" x 25"

Printed on glazed cotton muslin; commemorates Colorado statehood. Square surrounding wreath with large central star.

The thirty-eight-star flag representing Colorado statehood did not become official until July 4, 1877; however, the star count was widely used on flags a year earlier during the centennial celebration. Among the variety of designs created by flag makers were wreath patterns double medallions, Great Stars, squares, and various combinations thereof.

Flag size: 24" x 16"

13-STAR HALO FLAG • Ca. 1876

Printed on cotton. Haloed stars in wreath pattern with central star, flanked by star in each corner.

   This flag displays one of a number of innovative designs that flourished during the centennial period. The thirteen haloed stars are equal in size and pay tribute to the original thirteen states. Ex. Mastai collection.

Flag size: 16" x 11"

13-STAR JENNIE BACHMAN FLAG • Ca. 1876–79

Printed on glazed cotton muslin. Seven-pointed starburst pattern. Handwritten signature on top stripe reads:

Jennie Gail Bachman

   This starburst design is uniquely kinetic with its seven satellites appearing to be in motion around a ring of four stars with one central star. Perhaps the design of this flag comes closer than other patterns to the true spirit of the Flag Resolution adopted by Congress in June 1777 which specified "that the flag of the United States be thirteen stripes, alternate red and white; that the union be thirteen stars, white in a blue field, representing a new constellation."

Flag size: 5¾" x 4"

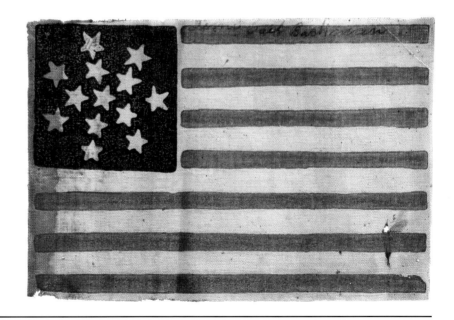

38-STAR GOLD FRINGE FLAG • Ca. 1876

Printed on silk with gold silk fringe on three sides. Four additional smaller stars inserted after second and third rows.

As the nation commemorated its one hundredth birthday, American flag makers used the occasion to create distinctive and unusual star patterns, as illustrated in this rare example with gold fringe.

Flag size: 27" x 21"

Civil War Remembrances

Following the end of the Civil War, veterans of the Union army formed groups to rekindle the friendships and camaraderie that had bonded them together and helped them survive the horrors of warfare. It was a time of mutual support as well as a time to remember the sacrifices of those who had fallen in battle.

Although state and federal leaders promised to provide for veterans, who needed jobs, and for the widows and orphans of those who did not return, little was done to keep those promises. Political pressure was necessary to ensure that disabled comrades and the families of those who died would not be forgotten.

The most prominent of the veterans' organizations was the Grand Army of the Republic (GAR), founded in 1866 by Dr. Benjamin F. Stephenson to provide fraternity, charity, and loyalty among former Union soldiers and sailors and to support legislation advancing benefits to veterans and their families. The national organization reached a membership of nearly half a million in 1890 with posts in every state and overseas.

Printed on glazed cotton muslin. Great Star pattern within wreath of stars. Handwritten note reads:

They are singing to my flag at a torchlight parade of Lincoln's men with their pick-axes and spades in 1864. As I stood on the porch waving this flag, the company of men opposite the house turned and saluted my flag and sang 'Rally Round the Flag Boys.'

Florence G.S.

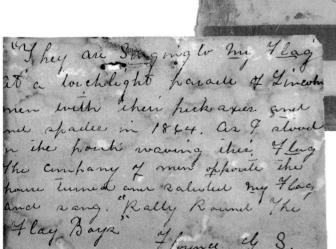

This flag is believed to be from a family member of the 24th Massachusetts Infantry Regiment. Organized at Camp Massasoit, Readville, in September 1861, the regiment saw extensive action in North Carolina, Virginia, Florida, and South Carolina before mustering out in January 1866.

Flag size: 17" x 12"

The 1st Rhode Island Cavalry Regiment organized at Pawtucket in December 1861 and mustered out in Baltimore in August 1865. The regiment served in Virginia with Sheridan's army, in the Shenandoah Valley campaign, at the battle of Gettysburg and in the defense of Washington.

Captain Bliss was awarded the Medal of Honor for heroic actions during the battle of Waynesboro, Virginia, September 28, 1864. He received three saber wounds, his horse was shot, and he was taken prisoner.

Flag size: 11" x 7"

Hand-sewn silk. Diamond pattern with embroidered gold stars; stripes in white and red sequence. Handwritten note reads:

Waved at the return of the 1st R.I. Reg, Capt. George N Bliss Commanding Officer. April 9, 1865. Made by Annie Francis Carpenter

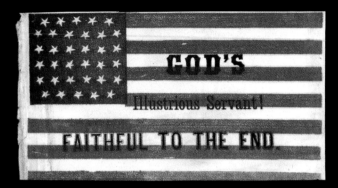

Flag size: 5½" x 3"

Flag size: 5½" x 3¼"

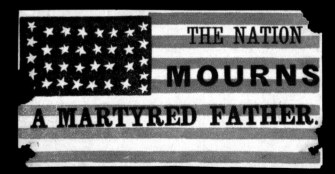

Flag size: 5" x 2¼"

Printed on paper. Various thirty-four-star patterns set upon black canton.

Flag size: 5" x 3½"

Flag size: 4½" x 3¼"

Overprints read:

> *God's Illustrious Servant*
> *Faithful To The End*
>
> *We Loved Him Living*
> *We Revere Him Dead*
>
> *We Mourn*
> *Our Chief Has Fallen*
>
> *The Nation Mourns*
> *A Martyred Father*

Abraham Lincoln, the sixteenth president of the United States, was shot by Confederate sympathizer John Wilkes Booth at Ford's Theatre on April 14, 1865. Lincoln was carried to a nearby boarding house and remained unconscious until his death the following morning. The assassination of the president plunged the nation into a period of deep mourning and transformed Lincoln into an American legend for his leadership during times of crisis and for his pursuit of a more perfect and equal union.

These are rare surviving examples of paper mourning flags printed for onlookers to wave during Lincoln's funeral procession.

Printed on cotton. Double medallion pattern, flanked by star in each corner. Overprint chronicles Civil War battles:

Bull Run   Fredericksburg   Chancellorsville   Gettysburg

The 71st New York Volunteer Infantry organized at Camp Scott, Staten Island, in June 1861 and mustered out in July 1864. The regiment was assigned to the 2nd Excelsior Brigade, under the command of General Daniel Sickles, which was part of General Hooker's division.

The regiment saw extensive battle action in Pennsylvania and Virginia. Sickles was awarded the Medal of Honor for his gallantry during the battle of Gettysburg.

When a regiment fought with distinction, the name of that battle was often inscribed on the stripes of the regimental flag. Battle honors were a source of great pride and added increased military significance to the flag.

Flag size: 24½" x 15½"

13-STAR JOHN MOSBY FLAG • Ca. 1876

Printed on glazed cotton muslin. Wreath pattern with central star, flanked by star in each corner. Notes written by Colonel John S. Mosby read:

> *On Bull Run we had enough cavalry to have taken Washington*
> *May 1, 1915 to William Dunn University of Virginia Cabal Hall*
> *From Col. Mosby*

John Singleton Mosby was born in Virginia in 1832. At the beginning of the Civil War, he enlisted in the 1st Virginia Cavalry but later joined Jeb Stuart's staff as a scout. His forays took him within the lines guarding Washington, with Mosby himself often doing the advance scouting in disguise. Wounded several times, he wreaked havoc among Union supply lines, disrupted communications, and took many prisoners.

Known as the "Gray Ghost," a nickname given him by President Lincoln following the bold capture of General Stoughton in 1863, Mosby was honorably paroled after the war by General Grant whose candidacy he later supported for the presidency.

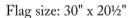 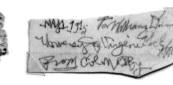

Flag size: 11½" x 7¼"

13-STAR MARIA LINES FLAG • Ca. 1895–1926

Machine-sewn wool. Naval ensign pattern. Inscription in selvage and below canton reads:

Mrs. M Lines

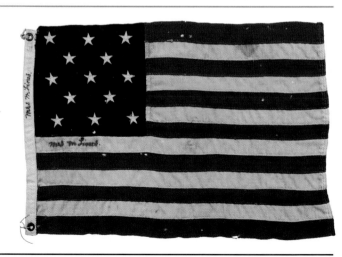

This flag was owned by Maria Lines, wife of Aaron Lines, a Civil War veteran who served with the 11th New Jersey Volunteers between August 1862 and May 1865. A member of Company B, Corporal Lines was taken prisoner in October 1863 during the retreat of Union troops led by General Pleasanton after the battle at Culpepper, Virginia. Lines would eventually be moved from Belle Isle to Andersonville in Sumter County, Georgia, where he survived the worst of conditions in that prison for more than a year before his release just before the end of the war.

Flag size: 30" x 20½"

Printed on glazed cotton muslin. Double medallion pattern with central star, flanked by star in each corner. Overprint reads:

Soldiers Monument
Dedicated To The Heroic Dead Of Camden Co., June 9, 1873.

The Soldiers' Monument was dedicated on June 9, 1873, in tribute to the memory of the 383 soldiers from Camden County, New Jersey, who died during the Civil War. The monument was unveiled with appropriate opening ceremonies and a number of dignitaries and a large crowd in attendance. On signal, a flag unfolded itself from around the monument base and ascended to the top of the flag pole as a shower of miniature flags fell gently upon the concourse below.

Flag size: 3½" x 2"

37-STAR GRANT PARADE FLAG • Ca. 1880

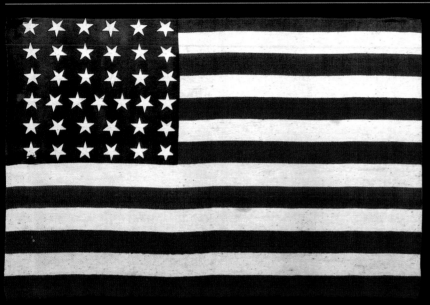

Printed on silk. Two handwritten notes accompany the flag, one of which reads:

In the fall of 1880, from the balcony of Roscoe Conklin's house in the city of Utica (John Street), Gen. U.S. Grant received a grand torch-light procession of the Republicans- a procession in which the students of Colgate (then Madison) University marched. When Gen. Grant's sharp eye caught sight of the large transparency that revealed the identity of our student company, his face was pleasantly lighted up, he uncovered his head, and graciously bowed, the boys enthusiastically rending the air with their college yell. I had this little flag with me in the procession. Many of the boys had brought them that day, and worn them as neckties. A man that fought so indomitably for the flag, ought to be saluted with it. So I saluted Grant with it. He has gone, but this flag is here. [signed] *Thos. Broxholm.*

Hiram Ulysses Grant was born in Point Pleasant, Ohio, in 1822. A West Point graduate and outstanding military figure, he served from 1869-77 as the nation's eighteenth president. Grant's middle name was "Ulysses," not "Simpson," as frequently reported; he admitted that the "S" in his name stood for nothing.

Flag size: 23½" x 15½"

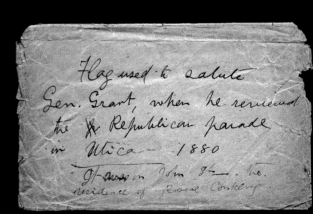

48-STAR BERDAN'S SHARPSHOOTERS REUNION FLAG • Ca. 1896

Printed on silk. Staggered pattern. Stamped overprint reads:

> *1896 July 29, 30 And 31. Berdan's U.S. Sharp Shooters*
> *At The Residence Of Eli Cook, Eaton Rapids, Michigan.*

At the beginning of the Civil War, Hiram Berdan, a New York engineer and inventor, proposed the formation of a special Union army organization of the best marksmen. Berdan was commissioned a colonel and given authority to form two regiments of sharpshooters. The units, known as the "Green Coats," distinguished themselves at Antietam, Chancellorsville, and Gettysburg.

Eli Cook served with distinction as First Sergeant of Company I, February 1862–January 1865. At the end of the war, he returned to Eaton County where, with his wife and three children, he devoted his life to agricultural pursuits.

Flag size: 6" x 4"

48-STAR 13TH NEW YORK REUNION FLAG • Ca. 1913

Printed on silk. Staggered pattern. Overprint stamped in gold reads:

> *13th N.Y. Inf. Vols. Blackburn's Ford, 1st Bull Run Smith's Mills Siege of Yorktown,*
> *W. Pt., Va. Hanover Court House, Mechanicsville Gaines Mills Savage Sta.*
> *Malvern Hill Second Bull Run, Antietam, Shepherdstown Fredericksburg*

The 13th Infantry Volunteers, the "Rochester Regiment," was organized under the command of Colonel Isaac Quinby in May 1861. Initially attached to Sherman's Brigade and later to the Army of the Potomac, the unit mustered out in May 1863. The regiment suffered sixty-three casualties and more than two hundred were wounded. This reunion flag commemorates the significant battles in which the regiment participated during its two years of active service.

Flag size: 5¾" x 4"

38-STAR 12TH NEW HAMPSHIRE REUNION FLAG • Ca. 1885

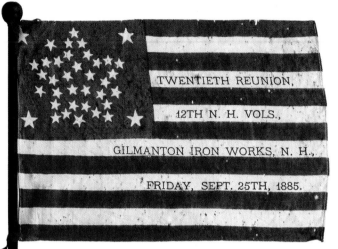

Printed on silk; original staff with red ribbon ties. Great Star pattern with four outlying stars, flanked by star in each corner. Overprint reads:

Twentieth Reunion, 12th N. H. Vols., Gilmanton Iron Works, N. H., Friday, Sept 25th, 1885.

The 12th New Hampshire Volunteer Infantry, "The Mountaineers," organized in September 1862 at Concord and mustered out in June 1865. The unit was initially attached to Casey's Division in the defense of Washington and later assigned to the Army of the Potomac. During its three-year tour of duty, the 12th was involved in thirteen military campaigns, including Gettysburg, Fredericksburg, and Chancellorsville, where it suffered its highest number of casualties.

This souvenir flag commemorates the regiment's twentieth Civil War reunion held in the town of Gilmanton Iron Works, New Hampshire, in 1885.

Flag size: 9½" x 6½"

42-STAR 7TH ILLINOIS REUNION GUIDON • Ca. 1889

Reunion guidon printed on silk. Double medallion pattern with central star, flanked by star in each corner. Stamped inscription reads:

*7th Illinois Cavalry G.A.R. Encampment
Camp Butler Illinois July 4th 1889*

The 7th Illinois Cavalry organized at Camp Butler near Springfield, Illinois, in October 1861 and mustered out November 1865. During its three years of service, the regiment engaged in battles at Corinth, Franklin, Nashville, and Vicksburg as part of the famous Grierson's Raid, a decisive victory that helped General Grant secure the last Confederate stronghold on the Mississippi River. The guidon commemorates the regiment's twenty-fifth encampment held at Camp Butler.

Flag size: 12" x 6½"

48-STAR SKELLY POST SOUVENIR FLAG • Ca. 1913

Printed on glazed cotton muslin. Staggered pattern. Overprint reads:

1863–1913 Compliments of Skelly Post # 9 Penna. Dept. G.A.R.

Corporal Johnston H. Skelly, a native of Gettysburg and member of the 87th Pennsylvania Volunteers, was engaged to Jennie Wade, who helped her sister bake biscuits and bread for Union troops. On July 3, 1863, while standing in the kitchen of her sister's home, Wade was killed when a bullet fired by a Confederate sharpshooter passed through two outer doors, hitting her in the back and piercing her heart. On the same day, Skelly was wounded at Carter's Woods, Virginia, and died nine days later. Neither ever learned the fate of the other. Jennie Wade was the only civilian killed in the battle of Gettysburg and the only civilian buried in the military cemetery there.

The flag commemorates the fiftieth anniversary of the battle of Gettysburg, fought July 1–3, 1863.

Flag size: 3½" x 2½"

42-STAR CONNECTICUT VOLUNTEERS REUNION FLAG • Ca. 1889

Printed on silk. Inscription on bottom white stripe reads:

Annual Reunion 10th & 20th Regs., Conn. Vol. Birmingham, Sept. 12, 1889

The 10th Volunteer Regiment mustered into service in September 1861 at Hartford and initially was assigned to Burnside's First Brigade and later to the Virginia campaign. The regiment engaged in battles from North Carolina to Florida and took part in the siege of Richmond and Appomattox. The regiment mustered out in September 1865.

The 20th Regiment was organized at New Haven and mustered into service in September 1862. During its three years of active service it was attached to the Army of the Potomac and the Army of the Cumberland. The regiment engaged in battles at Chancellorsville, Gettysburg, Atlanta, and Savannah, and mustered out in June 1865. This joint reunion of the two regiments was held in Birmingham, Connecticut, now known as Derby, a small town settled in 1651 at the juncture of the Housatonic and Naugatuck rivers.

Flag size: 17" x 11¾"

Printed on silk. Modified triple medallion pattern surrounding image of 1880 GAR membership badge.

The Grand Army of the Republic (GAR) was founded in 1866 by Dr. Benjamin F. Stephenson to provide fraternity among Union army veterans and to support legislation advancing benefits to them and their families. The national organization reached a membership of nearly half a million in 1890 with posts in every state and overseas. The last member, Albert Woolsen, died at the age of 109 in 1956.

The original GAR membership badge was manufactured in the form of a shield but was redesigned in 1869 with a ribbon and badge resembling the Congressional Medal of Honor. Its similarity to the Medal of Honor caused a great deal of controversy, necessitating a redesign of the eagle brooch again in 1880. GAR badges were struck from captured Confederate cannon metal, with the last believed to have been produced around 1940.

Flag size: 23½" x 15½"

48-STAR FOUR BROTHERS POST GAR FLAG
Ca. 1912–59

Printed on cotton. Vertical stamped overprint reads:

Four Brothers Post No. 453 G.A.R.

Named in honor of the four Lyons brothers who served in the Civil War, Four Brothers Post 453 was organized in Montrose, Pennsylvania, on September 4, 1884. Born to Nathan and Elizabeth Lyons, three of the brothers, Benjamin, Luke, and Clark, died during the war.

Captain Jerome Lyons, the only surviving brother, led the movement and was the architect who designed the Soldiers' Monument erected on the green in Montrose in 1876. Jerome died a year later from wounds received in battle. Monument Square, which lies between the courthouse and the county historical society, has four stone tablets on each side of the monument, each one identifying a township in Susquehanna County with the names of the men who served in the Civil War.

Flag size: 11½" x 17"

48-STAR HOOKER POST GAR FLAG • Ca. 1912–59

Printed on cotton. Overprint reads:

Joseph Hooker Post 23 G.A.R.

West Point graduate and native of Hadley, Massachusetts, Joseph Hooker was commissioned a brigadier general in 1861. During the next two years he commanded forces in the defense of Washington and in battles at Williamsburg and Antietam. Hooker was appointed commander of the Army of the Potomac and promoted to major general in 1863. During the battle of Chancellorsville, he was outmaneuvered by Confederate troops under Lee and Stuart, and was forced to retreat, suffering heavy losses. He finished out the war commanding the Ohio, Indiana, and Illinois sector before mustering out in September 1866.

Popular with men in the ranks, General Hooker turned his Army headquarters into a bordello, and the term "hooker" was coined to describe the prostitutes who followed the army under his command.

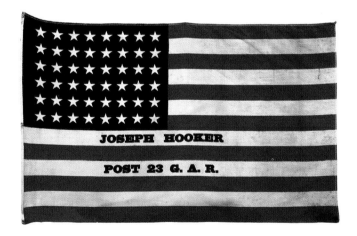

Flag size: 23" x 14"

40-STAR PEABODY POST GAR FLAG • Ca. 1889

Printed on glazed cotton muslin. Extremely rare star count. Overprint reads:

Everett Peabody Post No. 108   G.A.R. Georgetown, Mass.

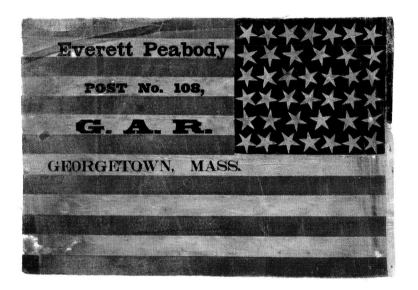

Colonel Everett Peabody commanded a brigade on the western flank of Grant's army at the battle of Shiloh. Fearing a Confederate attack, Peabody sent a reconnaissance force to strengthen their position, ordering his men to hold their ground if the enemy were encountered. Acting on his own, he hoped to provide a warning to the Union army in time to prepare for the coming onslaught. When the Confederates were engaged, Peabody and the rest of the brigade joined the battle. He was mortally wounded, but his heroic action surprised the enemy and eventually led to their surrender.

A Harvard graduate, Everett Peabody is among 136 alumni who gave their lives on behalf of the Union cause and are so honored in Harvard's Memorial Hall.

Flag size: 17" x 11"

45-STAR HOWELL POST GAR FLAG • Ca. 1896–1908

Paint-printed on cotton. Staggered pattern. Printed inscription reads:

Gen'l Howell Post 31 G.A.R. Woodbury, N.J.

Joshua Blackwood Howell was born near Woodbury, New Jersey, on September 11, 1806. Educated at the University of Pennsylvania, he was a lawyer and served in the state militia before the Civil War. During the war, Howell served with the 85th Pennsylvania Regiment in the defense of Washington and later commanded the 1st Brigade, Army of the Potomac, at Charleston. He died September 12, 1864, from injuries resulting from a fall from his horse. His death occurred two days before the orders arrived promoting him to brigadier general.

Howell's great grandfather, John Ladd, was hired by William Penn in the late 1600s to survey and lay out the city of Philadelphia.

Flag size: 16" x 11"

13-STAR LAFAYETTE POST GAR FLAG • Ca. 1860

Machine-sewn wool and hand-sewn cotton appliquéd stars. Third Maryland pattern. Inscription stamped in selvage reads:

Lafayette Post No. 140

To promote the spirit of patriotism, the Marquis de Lafayette GAR Post 140 presented an American flag to the City College of New York in June 1888. The goodwill and publicity surrounding this patriotic event inspired twenty-six other GAR posts in New York to undertake a statewide program of presenting flags to public schools during the 1890s.

Flag size: 25" x 16"

48-STAR GRANT POST ANNIVERSARY FLAG • Ca. 1916

Printed on silk. Staggered pattern. Inscriptions stamped in gold on satin streamers attached to the original staff read:

Gen. U.S. Grant Post 5 Dept. Pa. G.A.R. 50th Anniversary, 1866–1916

The Grand Army of the Republic (GAR), an organization of Union army veterans, was founded in April 1866 in Decauter, Illinois, by Dr. Benjamin Stephenson. The three cardinal principles of "fraternity, charity, and loyalty" comprised the GAR motto and guided its primary goals: to advocate veteran preference in job employment, provide assistance to needy members and their families, and encourage patriotic curriculum in the schools. The GAR also raised money to construct statutes and monuments honoring notable citizens as well as rank-and-file soldiers and sailors.

Flag size: 12" x 8"

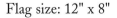

48-STAR PROBST PARADE FLAG • Ca. 1915

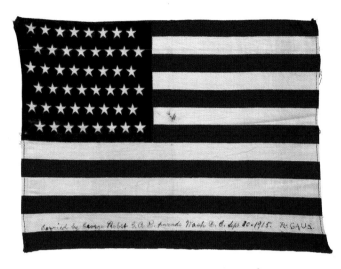

Printed on cotton. Staggered pattern. Inscription written on lower white stripe reads:

Carried By George Probst G.A.R. Parade Wash D.C.
Sept. 30, 1915 R. Gaus

Celebrating the fiftieth anniversary of the end of the Civil War, the Grand Army of the Republic marched from the Capitol to the White House passing in review before President Woodrow Wilson and receiving the plaudits of a quarter of a million people who lined Pennsylvania Avenue. There were 20,000 veterans in the long blue line, a small remnant compared to the number who marched before President Andrew Johnson a half century earlier.

America's highest-ranking government and military officials as well as many diplomats and ambassadors from other nations were present to pay tribute to the "boys in blue." In accordance with tradition, the procession was led by Illinois followed by the veterans of Pennsylvania, New York, and other departments in regular order.

Flag size: 16" x 11½"

48-STAR WOMEN'S RELIEF CORPS FLAG • Ca. 1912–59

Printed on cotton. Staggered pattern. Stamped overprint reads:

W.R.C. No. 85

The Women's Relief Corps was founded as an auxiliary of the Grand Army of the Republic in Denver in 1883 and incorporated by an act of Congress in September 1962. Organized into state and local chapters, the WRC initially limited membership to relatives of Civil War veterans. The WRC was established to care for disabled veterans and to help Civil War widows and orphans. Today its purpose is to honor those who have served our country in war and to promote patriotism by teaching the principles of citizenship.

The origins of this flag can be traced to Wiley Post No. 85, Bowling Green, Ohio, organized with forty-two charter members in June 1885 and ceasing activity in 1974.

Flag size: 16¾" x 11½"

Printed on cotton. Stamped overprint reads:

Gettysburg Blue And Gray Reunion
75th Anniversary Battle of Gettysburg 1938

A Blue and Gray Reunion commemorating the seventy-fifth anniversary of the battle of Gettysburg was held July 1-4, 1938. All living veterans of the Civil War received formal invitations to the event and were given free railroad passage. A special souvenir medal was struck for the occasion and presented to each of the 1,359 Union and 486 Confederate veterans in attendance.

This was the last Civil War reunion and the only time in history when all major veterans' organizations were assembled on a national stage. The lasting contribution of the reunion was the dedication by President Franklin Roosevelt of the Eternal Light Peace Memorial on the Gettysburg battlefield before a crowd of 450,000 visitors. Roosevelt spoke of the sacrifices, healing of wounds, and peace, but most strongly invoked the memory of Abraham Lincoln who chose the dedication of the Gettysburg Cemetery to deliver his famous address in November 1863.

Flag size: 23" x 14"

44-STAR POST 513 GAR FLAG • Ca. 1891–96
Printed on cotton. "Post 513 G.A.R." printed within outline of large central star. Colonel Dick White Post 513 in Hemlock, Pennsylvania. Flag size: 14" x 8½"

48-STAR POST 427 GAR FLAG • Ca. 1912–59
Printed on linen. Wreath pattern surrounding image of 1880-style GAR membership badge, flanked by star in each corner. "Post 427 G.A.R." stenciled on stripes. Flag size: 15¼" x 8¼"

48-STAR GRIMES POST GAR FLAG • Ca. 1912–59
Printed on cotton. Located in Hillsborough Bridge, New Hampshire, GAR Post 25 was named in honor of James W. Grimes, a U.S. Senator from Iowa who in 1861 introduced legislation establishing the Navy Medal of Honor. Flag size: 17" x 11"

48-STAR SHULER POST GAR FLAG • Ca. 1917
Printed on silk. The Sheridan, Wyoming, Post 67 was named in honor of John Shuler. Flag size: 16" x 14"

American Political Scene

Throughout the second half of the nineteenth century, politicians capitalized on the popularity of the Stars and Stripes by printing their portraits and campaign slogans on the American flag. Perhaps more than any other object or image, the flag was used to promote name recognition and bring attention to political issues of the day, with the intent of winning voter support. Candidates for public office believed that by identifying themselves with the flag they would be viewed as patriotic in the eyes of the electorate.

Today this practice is in violation of the Federal Flag Code, which prohibits the placement of any writing, pictures, or designs on the flag or the use of the flag for advertising purposes. Political candidates may display the flag at their campaign headquarters, in parades, and elsewhere, as long as the flag is not used improperly.

Printed on polished cotton. Pentagon pattern with outlying star, flanked by star in each corner. Overprint reads:

For President, John Bell. For Vice President, Edward Everett. The Union and the Constitution.

The Constitutional Union Party was formed in 1860 at a time of growing conflict over the issue of slavery within the Republican and Democratic parties. Comprised primarily of Whigs and Know-Nothings, the newly formed third party presented no election platform other than adherence to the Constitution, the Union, and enforcement of laws.

John Bell, presidential candidate for the Constitutional Unionists, was born in Nashville, served in the House and Senate, and was Speaker of the House and for a short time secretary of war under President William Harrison. His vice-presidential running mate, Edward Everett, was a Harvard professor, served in Congress, and was elected governor of Massachusetts.

In the election of 1860, Bell carried the states of Virginia, Kentucky, and Tennessee. He garnered more electoral college votes than Stephen Douglas, but both men lost by a wide margin to Abraham Lincoln.

Flag size: 11½" x 7¾"

36-STAR BLAINE 1884 CAMPAIGN FLAG • Ca. 1884

Printed on glazed cotton muslin. Image of James G. Blaine superimposed on stripes. Double medallion pattern with central star, flanked by two stars in each corner.

Blaine failed to win the Republican nomination for president in 1876 and 1880 but was successful in gaining his party's nomination in the election of 1884. The former Speaker of the House and secretary of state in the Garfield and Arthur administrations was a good family man and enjoyed strong support among immigrant groups, but apparently engaged in questionable investment schemes while on the public payroll. The campaign against Grover Cleveland was bitter and focused on each of the candidate's shortcomings. In a closely contested race, Cleveland edged Blaine to gain the presidency.

Flag size: 4" x 2¼"

36-STAR HARRISON 1888 CAMPAIGN FLAG • Ca. 1888

Printed on glazed cotton muslin. Great Star pattern within wreath of stars. Cotton band with name of presidential candidate Benjamin Harrison stenciled in black:

Harrison [letter "s" is reversed]

Throughout the latter part of the nineteenth century, politicians recognized the popularity of the Stars and Stripes and used the flag to promote their candidacy and political slogans during election campaigns.

This flag was used by Benjamin Harrison during the presidential campaign of 1888. In that election, Harrison received fewer popular votes than incumbent Grover Cleveland, but carried the electoral college to become the nation's twenty-third president. Ex. Mastai collection.

Flag size: 13" x 23½"

Printed on cotton. Image of Thomas Hendricks surrounded by wreath pattern, flanked by four stars in each corner. Legend on white stripe below canton reads:

Patented Sept. 4, 1883

Thomas A. Hendricks was the running mate of presidential nominee Samuel Tilden in the election of 1876, one of the most controversial in American history. Tilden won the popular vote, but a dispute over electoral college votes in Florida, South Carolina, and Louisiana resulted in the formation of a bipartisan commission, which by a straight party-line vote awarded the contested electoral votes to Rutherford B. Hayes, electing him president. Grover Cleveland chose Hendricks as his running mate in 1884, and the two narrowly defeated James Blaine and John Logan. Vice President Hendricks died in November 1885 after serving only nine months in office.

Flag size: 22" x 18"

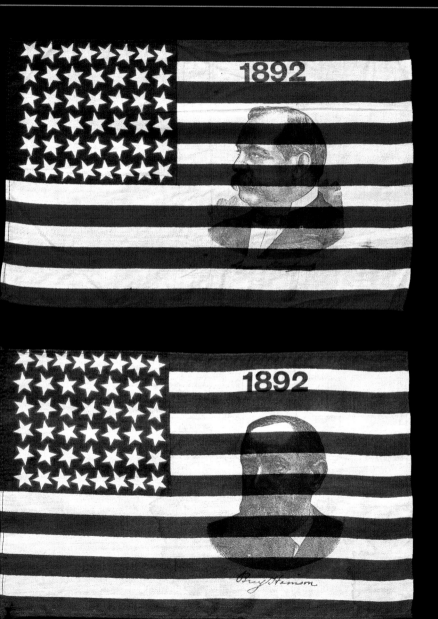

Printed on silk. Images and facsimile signatures of Grover Cleveland and Benjamin Harrison superimposed with stamped 1892 date.

Grover Cleveland was elected president in 1884, but lost his bid for reelection to Benjamin Harrison four years later, even though Cleveland won the larger popular vote. They faced each other again in the election of 1892, a contest dominated by the issue of tariff policies and one in which neither candidate led a unified party. Cleveland won handily, outpolling Harrison and third-party candidate James Weaver, and in doing so became the first president to serve two non-consecutive terms.

Flag sizes: 10¼" x 6½"

13-STAR SALEM PARADE FLAG • Ca. 1896

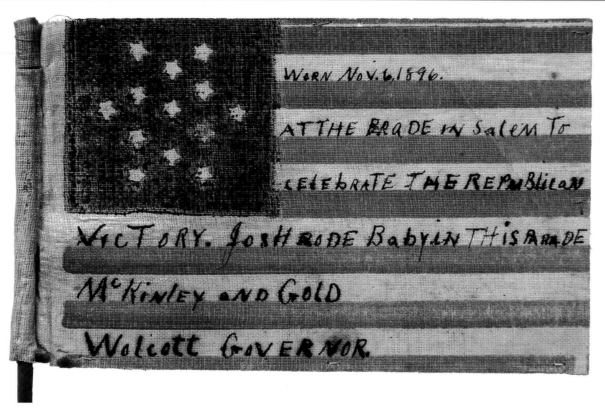

Printed on glazed cotton muslin. Six-pointed Great Star pattern. Handwritten inscription reads:

Worn Nov. 6, 1896. At The Parade in Salem To Celebrate The Republican Victory. Josh Rode Baby in This Parade. McKinley and Gold Wolcott Governor.

The election of 1896 was a contrast in styles between William McKinley, with his "front porch" campaign, and flamboyant orator William Jennings Bryan, who traveled across the country making speeches before large audiences. In the end, the voters chose Republican candidate McKinley, a strong supporter of the gold standard, by a convincing margin over Bryan, an advocate of the pro-silver movement.

Congress passed the Gold Standard Act in 1900, establishing gold as the only standard for redeeming paper money and putting an end to bimetallism, a monetary system based on both gold and silver. The gold standard was revoked in 1933 when the federal government feared the depletion of its gold supply during the Depression years.

Roger Wolcott was born in Boston in 1847 and, after graduating from Harvard Law School, served as a member of the state legislature. He was elected lieutenant governor in 1892 and succeeded Governor Frederic Greenhalge, who died in office. In 1896, Wolcott was elected governor and served three terms.

Flag size: 5" x 3"

48-STAR McKINLEY CAMPAIGN FLAG • Ca. 1901

Printed on glazed cotton muslin. Staggered pattern. Gold-painted inscription reads:

Flag Used In The McKinley Campaign Wellesley College 1901

Presiding over a period of prosperity at home and following the military victory over Spain in the Spanish-American War, President William McKinley easily won reelection against William Jennings Bryan in 1900. Six months into his second term, McKinley was assassinated by an anarchist while attending the Pan-American Exposition in Buffalo, New York. He died on September 14, and Vice President Theodore Roosevelt was sworn in as president.

McKinley and his cabinet visited Wellesley College for a Lincoln-Douglas debate celebration in 1899 and later campaigned there in the presidential election.

Flag size: 35½" x 19½"

45-STAR ROOSEVELT PRESENTATION FLAG • Ca. 1903

Printed on cotton. Irregular-shaped stars, staggered pattern. Inscription stamped in gold reads:

*Presented By The President Of The United States Theodore Roosevelt May 13, 1903
1919 California Street San Francisco.*

On May 13, 1903, during his three-day visit to San Francisco, President Theodore Roosevelt was greeted by thousands of cheering school children who lined the streets along his route to a reception at Native Sons' Hall, followed by a drive through the Presidio to review the militia under the command of General Arthur MacArthur. The president lunched at the famed Cliff House before returning through Golden Gate Park to the Palace Hotel.

This souvenir flag was presented at 1919 California Street, home of Michael H. DeYoung, who with his brother Charles founded the *San Francisco Chronicle* in 1895.

Flag size: 6½" x 4"

ONE HUNDREDTH ANNIVERSARY CELEBRATION OF THE

BIRTHDAY OF ABRAHAM LINCOLN, FEBRUARY 12, 1909

LINCOLN PARK CHAPTER, No. 177, R. A. M.

Printed on silk. Inscription reads:

One Hundredth Anniversary Celebration Of The Birthday Of Abraham Lincoln, February 12, 1909 Lincoln Park Chapter, No. 177, R.A.M.

Abraham Lincoln was born in Harden County, Kentucky, on February 12, 1809, to Thomas and Mary Hanks Lincoln. The family moved to Illinois when he was seven. Lincoln served in the state assembly and U.S. Congress and was elected president in 1860. Known as the "Great Emancipator," he was shot by John Wilkes Booth at Ford's Theatre on April 14, 1865, and died the following day.

This flag was printed by the Lincoln Park Chapter of the Royal Arch Masons (RAM) to commemorate the one hundredth anniversary of Lincoln's birth.

Flag size: 12" x 7¼"

44-STAR BRADLEY
INAUGURATION FLAG • Ca. 1895

46-STAR REPUBLICAN CLUB
FLAG • Ca. 1903

Printed on silk. Notched pattern. Inscription stamped on original staff reads:

Annual Dinner Of The Republican Club
Of Massachusetts March 3, 1903

Chartered by the Republican State Committee, Lieutenant Governor Eben Draper served as president of the Republican Club of Massachusetts during 1903–04.

Flag size: 17" x 11¼"

Printed on glazed cotton muslin. Notched pattern. Pencil inscription reads:

Carried In The Parade At Col Bradley Inauguration
At Frankfort Dec 10 1895

William O'Connell Bradley was born near Lancaster, Kentucky, in March 1847 and was educated by private tutors. At age fifteen he enlisted in the Union army but because of his youth served only a short time. He studied law, passed the bar examination when he was eighteen years old, and in 1870 was named prosecuting attorney of Garrard County.

In 1895, Bradley was elected Kentucky's first Republican governor, and the inscription on this flag commemorates the occasion of his inauguration in Frankfort. He served in the United States Senate from 1909 until his death in 1914.

Flag size: 11" x 7"

ANNUAL DINNER OF THE REPUBLICAN CLUB OF MASSACHUSETTS, MARCH, 3, 1908.

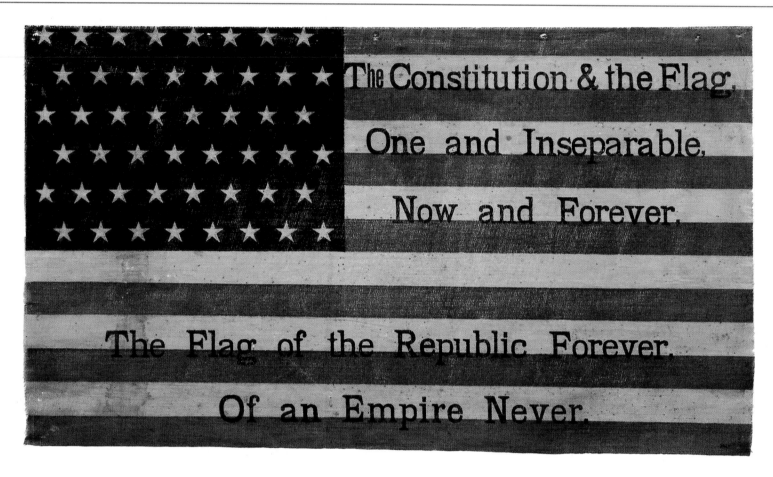

Printed on cotton. Staggered pattern. Overprint reads:

The Constitution & the Flag   One and Inseparable   Now and Forever
The Flag of the Republic Forever   Of an Empire Never

When Theodore Roosevelt became president in 1901, he further shaped the legacy of American expansionism inherited from William McKinley into a new imperialism. Roosevelt strongly believed in a new global role for the United States to match its growing economic power and interests. His antagonists, however, argued that such policies wrongfully imposed American values on others, and that global expansion did not advance civilization or peace but rather had disastrous consequences. This flag was used by opponents of Roosevelt during the election of 1912 when he unsuccessfully campaigned for president on the Bull Moose Party ticket.

Flag size: 23" x 13"

48-STAR WILSON SIGNATURE FLAG • Ca. 1912–20

Campaign flag printed on glazed cotton muslin. Signature "W. Wilson" stamped on stripes.

Woodrow Wilson was born December 28, 1856, in Virginia, the son of a Presbyterian minister. After graduation from Princeton and the University of Virginia Law School, he earned his doctorate degree at Johns Hopkins and began an academic career. He advanced rapidly as a conservative professor of political science and became president of Princeton University in 1902.

Wilson was elected governor of New Jersey in 1910, endorsing a progressive platform. His growing national reputation led to his nomination for president at the Democratic convention in 1912. Wilson defeated incumbent William Howard Taft and Teddy Roosevelt in a three-way race, capturing only 42 percent of the popular vote but an overwhelming majority of electoral college votes. He served two terms and died in February 1924, three years after leaving office.

Flag size: 6½" x 3½"

48-STAR TAFT ENVELOPE FLAG • Ca. 1908–12

Printed on silk. Staggered pattern. Inscription on accompanying envelope reads:

Don't Open Until President Taft Is Called Upon To Speak. Then Use It !

William Howard Taft was born in 1857 and after graduating from Yale University returned to Cincinnati to study and practice law. He rose in politics through administrative appointments, serving as chief civil administrator of the Philippines under McKinley and secretary of war in the Theodore Roosevelt administration. He was elected president in 1908, defeating William Jennings Bryan, but was unsuccessful in his bid for reelection in 1912.

It was during Taft's presidency that the size proportions and star arrangement of the United States flag were mandated by federal law.

This flag was folded inside an envelope and distributed to Taft supporters to wave at political rallies.

Flag size: 12" x 8"

DON'T OPEN UNTIL
PRESIDENT TAFT
IS CALLED UPON TO SPEAK

THEN USE IT!

Printed on glazed cotton muslin. Inscription reads:

Suffrage Parade June — 30 — 1914

In 1890, the two leading women's organizations of the time, one led by Elizabeth Stanton and Susan B. Anthony, and the other headed by Lucy Stone and Julia Ward Howe, merged to form the National American Woman Suffrage Association. Its agenda was to pressure state legislatures to amend state election laws and at the same time to pursue the adoption of a constitutional amendment for women's voting rights.

By 1914, Alice Paul and other activist leaders realized that full suf-frage would be achieved only through the adoption of a federal Constitutional amendment and that more militant action was necessary to strengthen their cause and give courage to friends of the movement. To this end, public parades, silent vigils, and hunger strikes were staged in large cities.

The "Anthony Amendment" passed both houses of Congress in 1918 and two years later was ratified as the Nineteenth Amendment to the Constitution.

Flag size: 6" x 4"

War and Peace

Since the time of the American Revolution, the United States has honored its servicemen and women and shown great respect for those who wear the uniform. A special holiday, named Veterans Day since 1954, is observed on November 11 with military ceremonies and speeches, and, at 11:00 in the morning, a moment of silence for those who made the ultimate sacrifice.

America's armed forces have fought in a number of wars to safeguard the nation's democracy and to bring freedom to others. Almost without exception, upon returning home these heroes have been met with victory parades and the admiration of a grateful nation.

The flag has played an important role in these celebrations, decorating streets and homes and waved by jubilant onlookers who lined parade routes in the towns and cities of the American landscape. The Stars and Stripes was always there to welcome back those who went to war to ensure a lasting peace.

Paint-printed on cotton. Wreath surrounding large eagle and colored shield, flanked by star in each corner.

In June 1782, Congress adopted the Great Seal of the United States featuring a bald eagle and shield with thirteen vertical white and red stripes. The eagle holds thirteen arrows in one talon, an olive branch in the other, and in its beak a scroll inscribed with the motto "E Pluribus Unum."

Following adoption of the Great Seal, there was a notable appearance of flags with an eagle painted on the canton. During both the War of 1812 and the Civil War, army regimental flags were produced with an eagle and the name of the regiment painted on a scroll beneath the shield. As America expanded into the western frontier, explorers carried eagle flags and presented them to Indian tribes as a symbol and expression of peace.

Flag size: 21½" x 14½"

35-STAR EAGLE FLAG
Ca. 1863–65

Printed on cotton. Wreath surrounding eagle holding scroll inscribed with motto "E Pluribus Unum," flanked by four stars in each corner.

Eagle flags gained popularity with the military after the adoption of the Great Seal in 1782 and were very much in evidence during the Mexican War and the Civil War. These flags were also carried as a symbol of peace by pathfinders who explored territories beyond the national boundaries of the United States in the mid-nineteenth century.

Flag size: 15½" x 10"

42-STAR 7TH CAVALRY PARADE GUIDON • Ca. 1889

Parade guidon printed on cotton. Stenciled overprint reads:

7 [crossed sabers] *US*

A guidon is a military flag or pennant carried by a cavalry company to identify its location on the battlefield and to signal troop movements. The size and shape of the usual regimental flag was not suitable for the mounted cavalry soldier; the swallowtail design enabled the colors to fly in the wind as the horseman galloped. Cavalry regiments carried guidons throughout the Indian campaigns in the west.

This guidon of the 7th Cavalry was used in ceremonies and parades at Fort Sheridan, Illinois.

Flag size: 24½" x 18¼"

13-STAR ESCORT FLAG • Ca. 1898

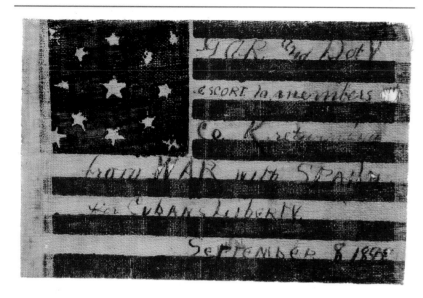

13-STAR THIRD MARYLAND PATTERN FLAG • Ca. 1848–6

Hand-sewn silk taffeta with linen sleeve and appliquéd stars. Wreath pattern with central star.

This design is often called the Third Maryland pattern because it is believed to have been used originally by a regiment of Maryland soldiers at the battle of Cowpens during the Revolutionary War.

Flag size: 26½" x 16"

Printed on glazed cotton muslin. Wreath pattern with central star, flanked by star in each corner. Inscription reads:

G.A.R. and D of V escort [10] members of Co. K returning from War with Spain for Cubans liberty. September 8, 1898.

Incorporated in Ohio in 1885, Daughters of Veterans was one of the nation's earliest women's direct-lineage societies organized to promote patriotism, to offer service in soldiers' and sailors' homes, and to honor veterans on Memorial Day. The organization changed its name to Daughters of Union Veterans of the Civil War (DUVCW) in 1925.

This flag likely documents a welcoming home celebration jointly sponsored by the Grand Army of the Republic (GAR) and Daughters of Veterans honoring troops returning from Cuba at the end of the Spanish-American War.

Flag size: 6" x 4"

Printed on glazed cotton muslin. Overprint reads:

Memorial Day. 1899.

In 1865, Henry Welles, a druggist in Waterloo, New York, came up with an idea to designate a special day for townspeople to place wreaths and flowers on graves of Civil War soldiers in the town cemetery. Coincidentally, similar ceremonies honoring those who died in the Civil War were being held in other regions of the country.

Originally established as Decoration Day, in May 1868 General John Logan, commander of the Grand Army of the Republic, proclaimed May 30 as a day to honor Civil War dead by placing flowers and wreaths on their graves in Arlington National Cemetery. After World War I, the annual ceremony was expanded to honor all armed forces personnel who died in America's wars. Congress declared Memorial Day a national holiday in 1971 and changed the day of observance to the last Monday in May.

Flag size: 13" x 9"

Printed on cotton. Inscriptions read:

Dewey NY Sept – 30- 1899

Admiral Dewey's Welcome   September 29th 1899
S.S. Miami Raymond & Whitcomb

George Dewey graduated from the Naval Academy in 1858 and served under Admiral Farragut during the Civil War. He rose to the rank of commodore in command of the Asiatic Squadron a few weeks before the start of the Spanish-American War. On April 27, 1898, he sailed on the flagship USS *Olympia* with orders to attack the Spanish at Manila Bay. Within six hours on May 1, he sunk or captured the entire Spanish Pacific fleet without the loss of a single American life. News of the victory made Dewey a national hero and, in March 1899, he was appointed admiral of the navy.

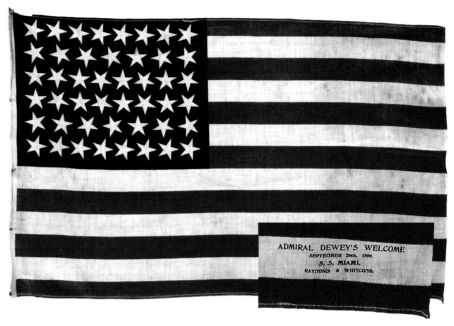

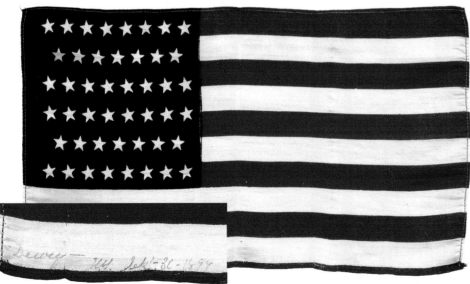

On September 27, 1899, Dewey returned to New York harbor for two celebrations: the naval parade on September 29 and the land parade on September 30. The events were filmed by the Edison Manufacturing Co.

One flag is a souvenir from the cruise ship SS *Miami*, among the hundreds of ships in New York harbor taking part in the Dewey naval parade. The ship was owned and operated by the Raymond & Whitcomb Cruise Line, headquartered in Boston. The other flag has ten stripes and commemorates the September 30 land celebration.

Flag sizes: (top right) 23" x 14½" (bottom left) 11" x 6¼"

48-STAR TANK CORPS FLAG • Ca. 1918

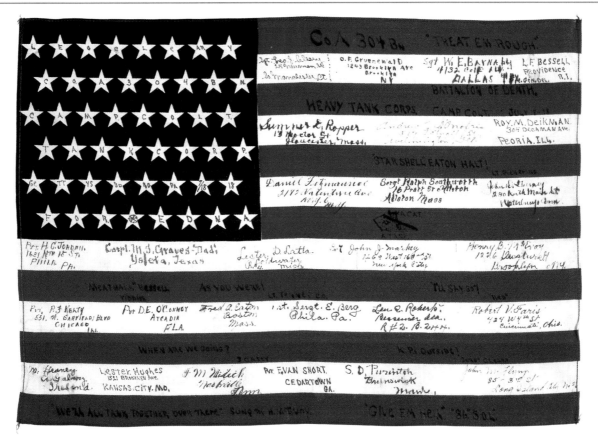

Printed on silk. Inscription on stars:

*Leo Cleary Co A 304 Bn Camp Colt Tank Corp Gettysburg Pa 7/18/18 For * Edna*

Handwritten on the stripes are notations along with the names and hometowns of several men in Company A.

The War Department established a military camp at Gettysburg in April 1917 to train members of the army in the use of armored tanks. Camp Colt, named for Samuel Colt, inventor of the revolver bearing his name, existed less than one year but was responsible for training more than 15,000 troops.

The commander of Camp Colt was Captain Dwight D. Eisenhower, who served from March to November 1918. Eisenhower had been identified as an officer with good organizational skills, and for that reason was assigned to command America's first tank training center. He was instrumental in establishing a separate armored unit known as the Army Tank Corps and for his efforts was awarded the Distinguished Service Medal.

Flag size: 14¼" x 10¼"

★ War and Peace ★   67

48-STAR KNOXVILLE PARADE FLAG • Ca. 1918

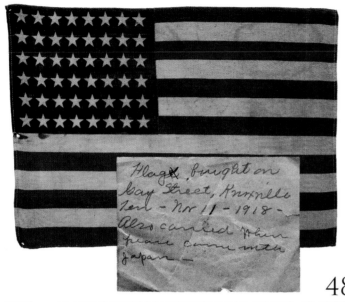

Printed on cotton. Accompanying note reads:

Flag Bought On Gay Street, Knoxville, Ten — Nov 11 — 1918 —
Also Carried When Peace Came With Japan —

At the end of the both world wars, parades were held in cities across the country honoring the return of American troops and celebrating world peace. Streets along parade routes were lined with cheering spectators waving American flags and watching soldiers and sailors in uniform march by to the sound of bands playing patriotic music. This was a time to rejoice and pay homage to the brave men and women who defended freedom against tyranny and brought an end to many years of armed conflict throughout the world.

Flag size: 16½" x 11½"

48-STAR 18TH U.S. INFANTRY FLAG • Ca. 1918

Printed on silk. Inscription on stripe reads:

18th US Infentry [sic]

The 18th Infantry Regiment was organized in New York in June 1917 and assigned to the First Expeditionary Division. In May 1918, it took part in the battle of Cantigny, the initial offensive action conducted by U.S. military forces against the Germans. The regiment was awarded two French Croix de Guerre with Palm and the French Fourragere for its part in the Soissons offensive and operations around Exermont.

The shoulder patch dates back to World War I. According to one of the legends about its origin, during the build-up and training days of 1917, an officer decided the division needed a suitable patch and cut a crude numeral "1" from his red flannel underwear, placing it on a piece of grey cloth from a captured soldier's uniform. In October 1918, a red "1" on a solid olive green background was the official patch approved for wear by members of the division. The First Division, known as the "Big Red One," is the oldest continuously serving division in the U.S. Army.

Flag size: 11¼" x 7¼"

45-STAR LONDON ARMISTICE DAY FLAG • Ca. 1918

Printed on cotton. Handwritten inscription in lower right corner reads:

Armistice Day! London. 11 Nov. 1918

At 11:00 a.m. on November 11, 1918, Germany signed a cease-fire agreement with the allied forces ending World War I. The eleventh hour of the eleventh day of the eleventh month has become a moment of special significance and honor associated with remembering those who died in the first modern world conflict.

In 1921, an unknown World War I American soldier was buried at Arlington National Cemetery in the Tomb of the Unknown Soldier. Similar ceremonies were held for soldiers in England and France. Armistice Day became a national holiday in 1938, and President Eisenhower signed legislation in 1954 proclaiming the holiday a day of remembrance of all wars and changing the name to Veterans Day.

In Great Britain, Armistice Day was renamed Remembrance Day after World War II and is celebrated on the second Sunday in November, usually the Sunday nearest November 11. Special services are held throughout England.

Flag size: 28" x 17½"

48-STAR VICTORY PARADE FLAG • Ca. 1918

Printed on cotton. Top red stripe removed. Ink inscription reads:

In Memory Victory Parade Dec. 7 1918 Given In Honor of Signing of Armistice Nov. 11, 1918 Which Stopped The World War For Democracy After 4 Years Of War.

The fighting in World War I ended on November 11, 1918, and in the months thereafter, as soldiers returned from Europe, parades were held in every city throughout America to honor their victory and to celebrate world peace. Large gatherings were highlighted by marching bands, the singing of patriotic songs, and tributes to the soldiers, sailors, and war workers for their efforts in winning the war and restoring democracy abroad.

Flag size: 14¼" x 8½"

48-STAR LIBERTY LOAN PARADE FLAG • Ca. 1918

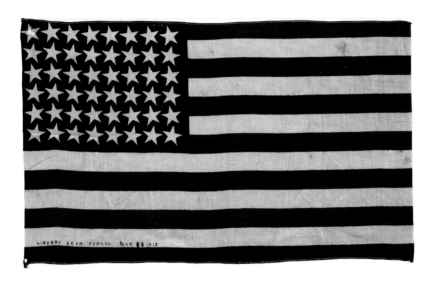

Printed on cotton. Ink inscription on bottom white stripe reads:

Liberty Loan Parade May 13 1918

When funds were needed to finance World War I, politicians and businessmen encouraged people to buy Liberty Bonds to help the country and support soldiers. The bonds were essentially a loan to the U.S. government which paid 4 percent annual interest until the debt was paid back. Purchase was considered both a patriotic gesture and a wise investment.

Four Liberty Loan bond parades and a variety of fundraising campaigns were held across the country. The War Industries Board, headed by Bernard Baruch, was able to raise $18.5 billion from bond sales during a two-year period.

Flag size: 23½" x 14"

48-STAR RED CROSS WORKER FLAG • Ca. 1918

Printed on silk. Handwritten note accompanying the flag reads:

Flag and ribbon I carried in the parade in 1918 the end of the World War. [signed] *Bertha as a Red Cross worker*

When the United States entered World War I, the American Red Cross turned its energies to supporting the needs of the thousands of young men joining the allied forces on the battlefields of Europe. Communities throughout the country flooded Red Cross headquarters with requests to establish local chapters, with the number growing to 3,700 and membership increasing to more than twenty million by the end of the war. In every community, the Red Cross called upon patriotic women to sew and knit for the boys in camps and overseas.

After the war, parades were held in cities across the nation celebrating the return of American troops and demonstrating the country's patriotic solidarity.

Flag size: 8" x 5"

Printed on silk. Wreath pattern with outer ring of stars surrounding six-pointed central star. The congressional circular signed by Wayne Whipple was sent to members of Congress before Flag Day, June 14, 1931.

Flag designer Wayne Whipple arranged the combination of stars in such a way as to make the stars record American history. The thirteen original states are in the center in the form of a six-pointed star, surrounded by a circle of twenty-five stars representing the states added to the union up to the time of the centennial in 1876, and an outer ring of stars representing additional states since the centennial.

Whipple called his flag the "Peace Flag" in tribute to the global peace movement during the years before World War I. Its design won a national contest in 1912 from among five hundred submitted entries and, although widely publicized, was never adopted.

Flag size: 24½" x 15"

Printed on cotton. Overprints read:

Remember Pearl Harbor Dec. 7, 1941

Keep 'Em Flying! Remember Pearl Harbor Dec 7 1941

Following the Japanese attack at Pearl Harbor, a resolute spirit of nationalism swept across America. Millions of men and women joined the armed services and fought valiantly on battlefields throughout Europe and the Pacific. On the home front, Americans worked in factories and shipyards to build the planes, tanks, ships, and other weapons needed to successfully wage war.

Patriotic items were produced with the motto "Remember Pearl Harbor" as a symbol of America's resolve in the war effort. The popular slogan "Keep 'em flying" was posted in aircraft plants to instill patriotism and invoked in flight-line pep talks to motivate pilots and crew, stressing the importance of working together to maintain air superiority.

Flag sizes: (top left) 5" x 4"
(bottom right) 16½" x 11¼"

48-STAR GOLD STAR MOTHERS FLAG • Ca. 1928–59

Printed on silk.

On June 4, 1928, a group of twenty-five mothers in Washington, D.C., led by Mrs. Grace Darling Seibold, founded a national organization known as the American Gold Star Mothers. Named after the gold star that families hung in a window in honor of a deceased veteran, membership was composed of mothers who lost a son or daughter during World War I. The organization offered mutual support for grieving mothers and loving care for veterans confined to government hospitals. Today there are more than two hundred chapters, and membership is open to mothers who have lost a son or daughter during past wars and armed conflicts, or while in the service of our country.

This presentation flag was given to Gold Star Mothers in New York City as an expression of appreciation and a symbol honoring their loss. When rolled up on its staff, the flag slips into a brass-tipped wooden tube for storage. The circular decal reads: "Presented to the Gold Star Mothers By the City of New York."

Flag size: 16" x 11"

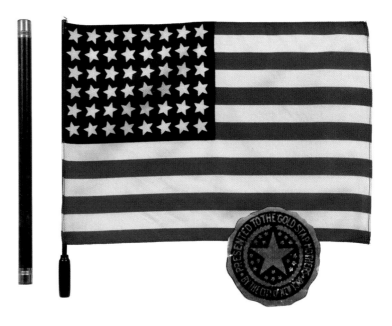

48-STAR JAPAN SURRENDER FLAG • Ca. 1945

Printed on cotton. Handwritten inscription reads:

Japan's Surrender Tues. Aug. 14, 1945 V-J Day Sept. 2, 1945

It had become evident during the early days of August 1945 that the time had come for Japan to surrender, yet the Japanese military hoped the coming invasion of its mainland would result in heavy losses of American forces, thereby making possible a more favorable negotiated peace.

On August 6, 1945, an atomic bomb was dropped on Hiroshima and, three days later, there was a similar bombing of Nagasaki. These events failed to induce Japan's military leaders to concede defeat, but their resistance was overcome by Emperor Hirohito's decision on August 14 to accept the terms of surrender and end the war. The actual surrender document was signed aboard the USS *Missouri* on September 2.

Flag size: 12" x 8"

48-STAR BERLIN CONVOY FLAG • Ca. 1945

Machine-sewn cotton and satin stripes with machine-embroidered stars.

On June 23, 1945, a U.S. military convoy entered Berlin to take control of the American sector of the city. In honor of the occasion, flags handmade in the nearby town of Halle were specially ordered for convoy vehicles. Colonel John J. McGinnis, a field officer involved with the army's military government operations, saved one of the flags as a souvenir of the historic event. He later bequeathed his flag to the National Museum of American History where it became part of the Smithsonian Institution exhibit *July 1942: United We Stand, The Flag In World War II.*

This is one of the original flags that was among the first to enter Berlin following the end of the Second World War.

Flag size: 14" x 10"

48-STAR BOYD PURPLE HEART FLAG • Ca. 1945

Printed on cotton. Inverted stars.

This flag was owned by Richard Boyd, a World War II paratrooper and Purple Heart recipient who was in London on May 8, 1945, for VE (Victory in Europe) Day and returned home with the flag. He is a member of York, Pennsylvania, Chapter 390 of the Military Order of the Purple Heart (MOPH), a service organization formed in 1932 for combat veterans who have received the decoration.

The Purple Heart was the first American military decoration given to the common soldier. Created as the Badge of Military Merit by General George Washington, it was presented to only three soldiers during the Revolutionary War, The medal was redesigned to include the profile of Washington and renamed the Purple Heart in February 1932 to coincide with the bicentennial of Washington's birth. At the same time, army regulations were revised authorizing the award to soldiers who received wounds in action against an enemy. A presidential order extended eligibility to the navy, marine corps, and coast guard in December 1941.

Flag size: 13" x 8½"

Stories on Flags

Whether describing an event or capturing a specific moment in time, flags with handwritten notations, signatures or stamped overprints and those accompanied by a personal note provide a snapshot from the past and a lasting footnote to the future.

Often it is the flag's story, its historical or social context, that is most fascinating. A flag waved at a parade honoring the return of our armed forces from war or noting an anniversary commemoration has special meaning and becomes a material part of the eyewitness account of the event.

In a sense we are fortunate to have examples that tell us stories about the past and give us insight into earlier periods of American history. The opportunity to do so no longer exists today because it is disrespectful to record such events or commemorate occasions on the face of the flag.

13-STAR HOP BITTERS FLAG
Ca. 1870-79

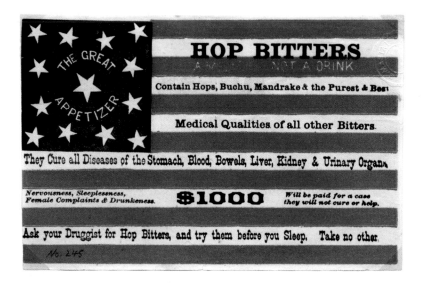

Advertising flag printed on paper. Wreath pattern with central star, flanked by star in each corner. Phrase "The Great Appetizer" surrounds central star.

During the 1870s, bitters became one of America's most popular medicines, purported to cure many diseases as well as purify the blood, regulate the liver and restore appetite and general health, all without intoxicating.

Bitters product advertising was among some of the best of the times, with manufacturers using a wide variety of gimmicks to promote their product, including almanacs, trade cards, tokens, decanters, and various other giveaways. Possibly this example is from Dr. Doyle's Hop Bitters Manufacturing Co. of Rochester, New York, which, like other patent medicine proprietors, did not hesitate to publicize its product across the face of the American flag. Ex. Mastai collection.

Flag size: 6¼" x 4¼"

36-STAR ROCHESTER SCHOOLS
FLAG • Ca. 1884

Printed on glazed cotton muslin. Stamped overprint reads:

Rochester Public Schools Semi–Centennial June 9th & 10th, 1884

The Rochester public school system was organized in 1834 into thirteen districts supervised by appointed trustees; however, the quality of instruction, facilities, and the number of months school was in session depended on the funding resources of each district. After two years, a citizens' committee recommended the establishment of a free public school system supported by a general tax on real and personal property. In 1841, Rochester became the fourth city in New York and one of the first in the nation to adopt what was considered at the time such a radical social measure.

Flag size: 5¼" x 9¼"

38-STAR EASTHAMPTON CENTENNIAL FLAG • Ca. 1885

Printed on cotton. Stenciled overprint and handwritten inscription reads:

1785 June 1885 Easthampton, Mass.

From the time of its first settlement in 1664, Easthampton remained within the boundaries of Northampton and Southampton until June 17, 1785, when Governor James Bowdoin approved legislation establishing it as a separate district. Easthampton was incorporated as a town replacing the district organization in June 1809.

On June 17, 1885, Easthampton commemorated its one hundredth anniversary with an elaborate celebration that included a parade through town and the reading of a poem specially written for the occasion. That evening a fireworks display and open-air concert concluded the festivities.

Flag size: 18" x 12"

27-STAR ALEXANDER THE GREAT FLAG • Ca. 1874–94

Printed on glazed cotton muslin. Diamond pattern. Handwritten inscription on top selvage reads:

Herr Alexander the Great Magician

Alexander Herrmann was born in Paris in 1844. At age ten he joined his brother Carl, a successful sleight-of-hand artist touring Europe and the United States. He remained his brother's assistant for six years while he began his own career as a magician.

Known as Alexander the Great, Herrmann was the first American superstar of magic, setting the standard for show business magicians. The varied menu of his shows included card tricks, items produced from thin air, live animals, and levitation and vanishing. His trademark goatee and evening attire made his character as magician a recognizable showbiz figure to all. Herrmann died in December 1896. During his lifetime he made and lost several fortunes primarily through theatrical speculations.

This flag was produced as early as 1845, but not autographed until decades later, perhaps in connection with an anniversary or special event. Ex. Whitney Smith collection.

Flag size: 4¼" x 3¼"

Printed on glazed cotton muslin. Wreath pattern with oversized stars, flanked by star in each corner. The notation "4th" handwritten within central star. Inscription reads:

Given to Edna Gardiner July 4 1891
by Allie May Ishorn
Remember me Allie May

The persons noted on this flag and the reason it was given as a remembrance are unknown. Perhaps there is some association with Wyoming statehood since July 4, 1891, was the date the forty-fourth star, representing Wyoming, was added to the official American flag.

Flag size: 7" x 4½"

44-STAR JOHN DREW FLAG • Ca. 1892

Printed on silk. Overprint reads:

John Drew 100th Standard Theater December 28th 92

John Drew Jr. (1853-1927) was born in Philadelphia, the eldest child of parents who were both performers and owned a theatre. In 1875, Drew joined a Shakespeare company and performed in a number of plays until 1892 when he starred in modern comedies. His sister Georgiana married Maurice Barrymore, uniting two distinguished families of the stage; their children were Lionel, Ethel, and John.

This flag celebrates the one hundredth performance of John Drew in *The Masked Ball* at the Standard Theatre (later named Manhattan Theatre) in New York City. The play also starred Maude Adams. Ex. Mastai collection.

Flag size: 10½" x 6¾"

13-STAR FLAG DAY FLAG
Ca. 1892

Printed on glazed muslin. Wreath pattern with central star, flanked by star in each corner. Initials "APA" handwritten within central star. Inscription reads:

Dist. No 1. Flag Day. October 11, 1892

As part of the ceremonies marking the four hundredth anniversary of Christopher Columbus's discovery of America, on October 11, 1892, the Pledge of Allegiance was recited for the first time by more than twelve million children in schools across the nation. Authored by Francis Bellamy, the pledge was anonymously published a month earlier in the *Youth's Companion*, a family magazine. There have been several changes over the years, with the present wording adopted on June 14, 1954.

June 14 was proclaimed Flag Day by President Wilson in 1916, but it was not until August 1949 that Congress passed legislation designating that date as National Flag Day.

Flag size: 5¾" x 3½"

13-STAR FLAG ON ENVELOPE
Ca. 1893

13-STAR MAINE FESTIVAL FLAG
Ca. 189

Printed on glazed cotton muslin. Wreath pattern with central star, flanked by star in each corner. Inscription reads:

Maine Festival — 1897.—

The Maine Music Festival, a series of concerts throughout the state, was organized in 1897 by William Rogers Chapman and continued for more than a quarter of a century as one of the foremost annual musical events in America. Chapman directed the festival for many years and was responsible for bringing some of the nation's best musicians and performers to his hometown of Bethel, Maine, each summer to perform.

Flag size: 7" x 4¼"

Printed on glazed cotton muslin. Wreath pattern with central star, flanked by star in each corner. Affixed two-cent 1893 Columbian Exposition stamp with post office cancellation. Handwritten address reads:

For Miss Emily Bosworth — Florence Mass. C/of Uncle Sam

This flag was folded around a post card, sealed with red wax to form an envelope, and mailed through the postal system. The cancellation is not completely legible but it appears to have been mailed on July 4, 1893, at 6:00 p.m. from Stonington, Maine. A two-cent Columbian Exposition stamp issued in January 1893 was used for postage. Ex. Mastai collection.

Flag size: 7½" x 4½"

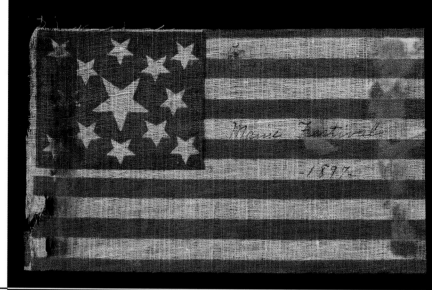

44-STAR SUNDAY SCHOOL FLAG • Ca. 1895

Printed on glazed cotton muslin. Notched pattern. Typewritten inscription reads:

Sunday School Rally At Christian Church, Cameron, Mo January 6, 1895. God Bless Our Flag! Long May It Wave. O'er The Land Of The Free And The Home Of The Brave.

Rally Day traditionally celebrates the annual enrollment of children, youth, and adults in Sunday School classes and the involvement of the congregation in other church activities.

This flag was used in a unique way to announce the commencement of Sunday School classes and at the same time to pay homage to the Stars and Stripes.

Flag size: 9½" x 6"

45-STAR EDEN PARK FLAG • Ca. 1896-1908

Printed on glazed cotton muslin. Notched pattern. Handwritten inscriptions read:

Souvenir of the flag-raising in Eden Park
[selvage] *Souvenir of the flag*

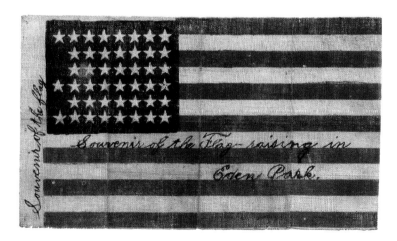

Eden Park was created in 1859 as part of Cincinnati's park system, and today it is the city's largest and most popular recreational facility, combining culture, city history, and notable architecture. Named after the Garden of Eden, the park is home to the Cincinnati Art Museum, Playhouse in the Park, and the Krohn Conservatory.

Five memorial tree plantings throughout the park honor U.S. presidents, Revolutionary War heroes, Cincinnati men and women who lost their lives in World War I, Cincinnati pioneers, and authors. The water tower and Melan Arch Bridge, both completed in 1894, are two of the many architectural landmarks.

Flag size: 8" x 4½"

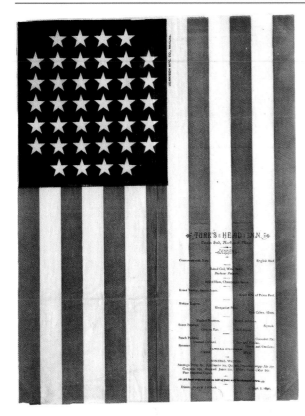

38-STAR PAPER MENU FLAG Ca. 1890
Printed on paper. Notation "Dennison Mfg. Co., Makers" printed on white stripe below canton. This paper flag is the dinner menu from the Turk's Head Inn, Land's End, Rockport, Massachusetts, on September 2, 1890.

Flag size: 13" x 17¼"

42-STAR PAPER MENU FLAG
Ca. 1888
Printed on paper. This is the dinner menu from the Bass Rock, Gloucester, Massachusetts, on Thursday, August 30, 1888.

Flag size: 13" x 17¾"

48-STAR MENU FLAG • Ca. 1904
Printed on satin ribbon. Fourth of July dinner menu from the Hotel Alleesaal in Langen-Schwalbach, Germany in 1904. Ex. Mastai collection.

Flag size: 8" x 5"

Printed on cotton. Staggered pattern. Handwritten notations read:

*Ezekiel Morse 19 Hastings St. Lowell Mass. John A. Hunt
Providence RI July 4th , 1899 Hattie S. Sawyer #4 Maple Pl.
Lowell, Mass. Aaron C. Sawyer Lowell Mass. Age 80 Years
July 3rd 1899 Edith L. M. Harlon #3 Maple Pl. Lowell, Mass.
Mrs. James A.F. Merley Blanche L. Merley #3 Maple Place*

Lowell Mass. Mr. James A Merley

Possibly this flag was signed by family and friends to
commemorate the eightieth birthday of Aaron Sawyer during
the July 4 holiday in 1889.

Flag size: 17½" x 11¾"

45-STAR BESSIE ERVIN FLAG
Ca. 1900

45-STAR MT. VERNON TRAMP FLAG • Ca. 1901

Printed on cotton. Staggered pattern. Pencil inscriptions on stripes record comments of participants after ten-mile hike at Mt. Vernon, New York, on October 10, 1901.

A group of friends completed a hike at Mt. Vernon and, as a memento of the occasion, each wrote a personal message and signed his name on the flag.

Flag size: 23¾" x 14¾"

Printed on glazed cotton muslin. Staggered pattern. Inscription reads:

Bessie Ervin 1900 Centennial Oct. 5-7

This flag was owned by Bessie Ervin and commemorates the one hundredth anniversary of the founding of Johnstown, Pennsylvania. According to information provided by a member of her family, Bessie, born September 27, 1889, was the oldest of ten children. The history of the Ervin family in Johnstown dates back several generations to the Revolutionary War period.

On June 1, 1889, Johnstown was devastated by the worst flood in the nation's history. Over 2,200 died and many more were left homeless.

Flag size: 10¼" x 6¾"

38-STAR YPSCE FLAG Ca. • 1881–90

Printed on glazed cotton muslin.
Inscription on stripe below canton reads:

YPSCE

The Young People's Society of Christian Endeavor (YPSCE) movement was founded in 1881 by Francis E. Clark at the Williston Church in Portland, Maine. Its purpose was to involve youth in the church and Christian life through activities and opportunities for service. The movement spread rapidly throughout the United States and the rest of the world. Clark retired from active leadership in 1925 and was succeeded by Dr. Daniel A. Poling, a well-known minister, platform speaker, and leader in young people's activities.

The organization moved its world headquarters from Boston to Columbus, Ohio, in 1952. Still operating today, its principal success has been among Protestant churches.

Flag size: 33½" x 20"

46-STAR BALTIMORE SAENGERFEST FLAG • Ca. 1903

Printed on silk. Stenciled overprint reads:

Baltimore 1903 S'ngerfest Inaugural Concert June 14

Clubs and associations among immigrant communities in America provided a social outlet and helped members adjust to an unfamiliar cultural environment. One such organization was the German singing society, or "Gesangverein."

Its history in the United States began with the founding of a men's choir in 1835 in Philadelphia, followed a year later by a group in Baltimore. Over the next several years many other groups were formed, and soon these societies began to hold joint concerts called "Sangerfests," or singing festivals, hosted by clubs in various cities. By the end of the century, the event expanded to a week-long celebration with picnics and parades and special prizes awarded for competitive singing. In 1935 women's choruses were added. The festival held in Baltimore at the Hutzler Palace in June 1903 was highlighted by a speech by President Theodore Roosevelt.

Flag size: 17¾" x 11¼"

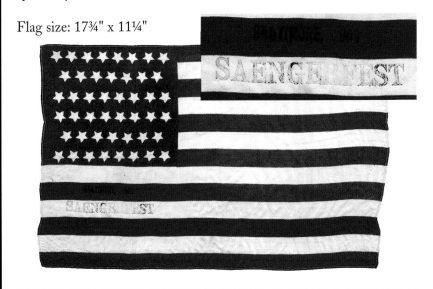

48-STAR BASEBALL GAME FLAG
Ca. 1903

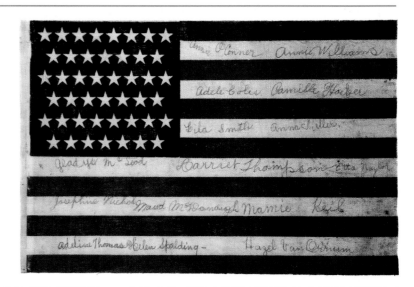

Printed on glazed cotton. Staggered pattern. Handwritten inscriptions on both sides of flag read:

> [Obverse] *Fireworks at Harlows G.B.S. & S.A.W. H.A.H.& A.B.W. Went July 4, 1903. Ball game 6 to 4 in favor of Kingfield.*
> [Reverse] *July 4, 1903. H.A.H. Ball game between Lexington & Kingfield, 6 to 4 in favor of Kingfield.*

Since the earliest days of the republic, Americans have observed the anniversary of the nation's independence as a major holiday and celebration. Many of today's Fourth of July traditions — fireworks, parades, and games —have their roots in local customs dating back to the post–Revolutionary War period.

The written notations on this flag recount the July 4 fireworks celebration and score of a baseball game possibly played between the neighboring towns of Kingfield and Lexington, Maine, at the Harlow family farm in 1903.

Flag size: 7½"x 4½"

45-STAR WISHART SIGNATURES FLAG • Ca. 1896–1908

Printed on glazed cotton muslin. Name "E Wishart" embroidered on top red stripe followed by signatures:

Annie O Connor Annie Williams Adele Coles   Camille Hoelzer Lila Smith Anna Miller Gladys McLeod Harriet Thompson Etta Naylor Nellie Egan L Barr Josephine Nichol Maud McDonough Mamie Keil Adeline Thomas Helen Spalding Hazel Van Ornum

The origin or purpose of this flag is forever lost in time and history. Perhaps it was a special award presented by an organization or women's group in honor of one of its members or possibly a memento of a special event that was signed by those in attendance.

Flag size: 18" x 12"

Printed on paper.
Supplement to the
Boston Sunday Post.
Notation under flag reads:

> *Directions: thoroughly
> moisten a piece of thin
> white cloth on which you
> wish to transfer the flag,
> place it over the printed
> side of this supplement,
> then place a few thick-
> nesses of paper over the
> cloth and rub hard with
> a crumpled cloth or
> handkerchief until
> the color shows through
> the cloth.*

Founded in 1831, the *Boston Post* was the most popular newspaper in New England and one of the largest in the country for more than a hundred years. Increased competition from other newspapers and from radio and television in the 1950s caused declines in circulation, and inevitably the paper closed its doors in 1957.

Flag size: 10" x 7"

45-STAR BOY SCOUT FLAG
Ca. 1914

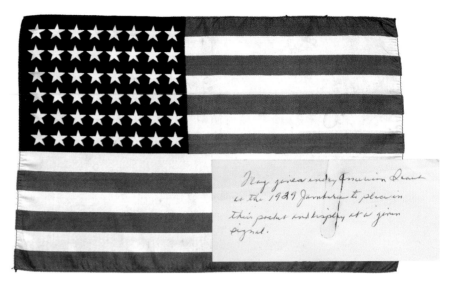

48-STAR BOY SCOUT
JAMBOREE FLAG • Ca. 1929

Miniature flag printed on paper. Staggered pattern.
Overprint reads:

To Help Buy a Flag For Our Boy Scout Troop

In 1914, the Dean Flag Company of Cincinnati, Ohio, one of the world's largest flag manufacturers, sponsored a program to help Boy Scouts acquire an American flag for their troop. By selling twenty of these miniature flags for ten cents each and remitting the $2.00 to Dean, the scout troop would receive a wool bunting forty-eight-star flag. According to the manufacturer, each flag was of the same quality as those used by the federal government and guaranteed not to fade or run.

Flag size: 1¼" x 1¾"

Printed on silk. Accompanying handwritten note reads:

*Flag given every America Scout at the 1929 Jamboree
to place in their pocket and display at a given signal.*

The Third Boy Scout Jamboree was held at Arrowe Park, Birkenhead, England, in the summer of 1929 with fifty thousand scouts from forty-one nations participating. This assemblage of scouts from around the world was known as the "Coming of Age Jamboree" because it marked the twenty-first anniversary of scouting.

Opening day ceremonies were highlighted by the parade of nations, in which each scout passed the viewing stand and was greeted by the Duke of Connaught and chief scout and founder of the Boy Scout movement, Lord Robert Baden-Powell. As the American contingent passed the stand, the flags that led the way were dipped in salute and every scout waved a miniature Stars and Stripes.

Flag size: 17" x 11¼"

Printed on cotton. Staggered pattern. Handwritten inscription reads:

On board the 'Amerika' Aug 12th 1909 [with signatures of seventeen ship passengers and address or home town]

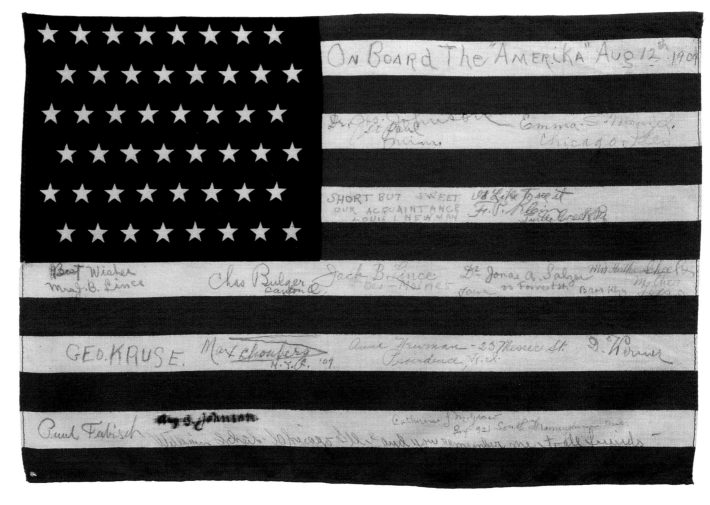

The German passenger liner *Amerika* embarked on its maiden voyage from Hamburg to New York in October 1905. The ship offered superior service and luxurious traveler accommodations. In spite of its many technological innovations, the ship was involved in a number of at-sea incidents, including one on April 10, 1912 (the same day as maiden voyage of the *Titanic*), when the *Amerika* rammed and sank a British submarine off the coast of Dover.

In 1917, the ship was seized by the U.S. Navy, commissioned the USS *America*, and converted to a troop transport. After the war, the ship was rebuilt and served as a passenger liner until 1943 when it was reactivated as the U.S. Army transport *Edmund B. Alexander*. The ship was sold for scrapping in January 1957.

Flag size: 17" x 11½"

Printed on silk. Accompanying card reads:

> *Welcome To Citizenship*
> *Allied Patriotic Women's Societies*
> *Of Brooklyn*

A flag and information card containing "The Code of Courtesy to the Flag" and "Your Oath of Allegiance" distributed to new citizens.

Flag size: 10" x 7"

WELCOME TO CITIZENSHIP

———

ALLIED PATRIOTIC WOMEN'S SOCIETIES

OF

BROOKLYN

YOUR OATH OF ALLEGIANCE

———

I hereby declare, on oath, that I absolutely and entirely renounce and abjure all allegiance and fidelity to any foreign prince, potentate, state or sovereignty and particularly to **the one** of whom I have heretofore been a subject; that I will support and defend the Constitution and laws of the United States of America against all enemies, foreign and domestic; and that I will bear true faith and allegiance to the same.

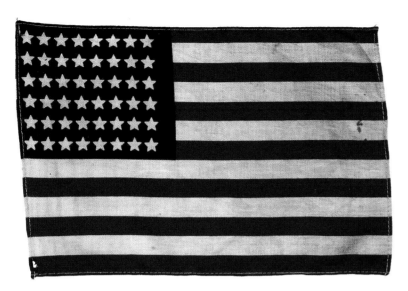

SOUVENIOR OF ST MARY'S JUNIOR DANCE JAN. 29, 1938

48-STAR ST. MARY'S DANCE FLAG • Ca. 1945

Printed on cotton. Notation on staff reads:

Souvenior [sic] *Of St. Mary's Junior Dance Jan. 29, 1938*

Flag size: 11" x 7½"

48-STAR CRÉME SIMON FLAG • Ca. 1945

Printed on paper. Overprint reads:

Vivent Les Allies Créme Simon Soins De La Peau

A patriotic advertising flag distributed at the end of World War II as a tribute to the American armed forces for their role in liberating France from occupation by the Germans.

Flag size: 3" x 2"

13-STAR COLUMBUS DAY FLAG RIBBON • Ca. 1892

In 1891, James Upham, an owner of the *Youth's Companion* magazine, conceived the idea of promoting a flag-raising ceremony at every public school as part of the planned celebration of the four hundredth anniversary of Christopher Columbus's discovery of America. Francis Bellamy, a member of the *Youth's Companion* staff, wrote the official program for the celebration including a flag salute, the original Pledge of Allegiance.

Ribbon size: 2" x 4"

13-STAR ALCOTT FLAG RIBBON • Ca. 1892

Local groups of the Daughters of Union Veterans of the Civil War (DUVCW) were called tents and named for Civil War nurses and other patriotic women. Louisa M. Alcott Tent 8 was founded in Fitchburg, Massachusetts, in 1892 and disbanded in 1924. Alcott served as a nurse for a short time during the Civil War.

Ribbon size: 2¼" x 4"

13-STAR MT. OLIVER SCHOOL FLAG RIBBON • Ca. 1906

Mt. Oliver, Pennsylvania, is a small suburb of Pittsburgh and part of the same school district. This flag ribbon commemorates the anniversary of the public school in town.

Ribbon size: 2¼" x 4"

13-STAR SONS OF VETERANS FLAG RIBBON • Ca. 1898

The thirty-second GAR reunion was held in Cincinnati during September 5-6, 1898, with an estimated crowd of 400,000, including veterans and their families and friends. In 1881 the GAR formed the Sons of Veterans (S of V) to carry on its traditions. Since 1925, when the name was changed to Sons of Union Veterans of the Civil War (SUVCW), this organization has been recognized as successor to the GAR.

Ribbon size: 4" x 2"

ABOUT THE COLLECTION

What was a thirtieth wedding anniversary gift has turned into a cornerstone of one of America's most extensive parade flag collections. That thirteen-star flag, a hand-sewn classic dating from the nation's centennial celebration, was the first in what now ranks as one of the premier collections of its kind in the country.

This collection of American parade flags encompasses a wide variety of unusual star patterns, including single wreath or medallion, double medallion, Great Star, diamond, global, pentagon, square, and scattered configurations. Other representative examples incorporate an eagle or haloed stars within the canton. Several flags are one of a kind, hand-sewn during the Civil War and centennial periods.

Among the earliest and rarest are two twenty-six-star flags printed on homespun cotton that date to circa 1837, one a great star pattern and the other a double medallion with a large central star. Few are known to exist today. Other rare examples include five Lincoln mourning flags printed on paper, an anti–Teddy Roosevelt campaign flag from the 1912 presidential election and a number of great star pattern flags. Two flags dating from the first half of the nineteenth century are a hand-sewn fourteen-star flag that starts with a white stripe and has a full-width canton, and a twenty-four star flag made from silk. Many are extremely rare because of their unique star pattern; examples are the hand-sewn thirty-five-star silk flag with an embroidered diamond pattern, and a hand-sewn thirteen-star centennial flag with a single wreath surrounding a triangle of appliqued stars. Two eagle flags and a Whipple peace flag are also examples of rare and unique star configurations.

Of equal interest and importance are flags with handwriting on them or stamped overprints, and flags that were found with personal notes or other documents that capture a specific moment or describe a special event, a snapshot of history, so to speak. More than half the flags in the collection have some form of overprint or inscription, including many related to political campaigns, the Grand Army of the Republic, Civil War reunions, July Fourth celebrations, special anniversary commemorations, military endeavors, menus, and advertising.

Early parade flags were generally made to wave at a special celebration, parade, holiday event, or political rally, and then to be discarded, which explains why only a small number has survived through the years. They range in size from a few inches to less than three feet in length, and most were printed on cotton; some are on glazed muslin and others on silk or paper.

As of this writing, there are more than two hundred flags in the collection, most of which were acquired during the past five years. Some were obtained at auctions and antique shows, but most were purchased from the country's two leading antique American flag dealers.

Each flag is stitched with archival thread to an acid-free mat board and, in most cases, placed in a museum-quality period or gilt frame. Spacers around the perimeter of the frame keep the fabric from touching the ultraviolet protective glass. If a silk flag has thread separations and is extremely fragile, usually it is pressure-mounted with Acrylie, an acid-free acrylic, to maintain stability and preserve its condition.

Several flags were exhibited as part of an American flag exhibition at the Heart of Country antiques show in Nashville and also at the Blackwells Mills Canal House museum in Franklin Township, New Jersey, during 2002. A major exhibition of the collection was part of the Journey Fourth commemoration of the Lewis and Clark Bicentennial celebration in Atchison, Kansas, in July 2004. *The Stars and Stripes: Fabric of the American Spirit* exhibition was on display at Hancock Shaker Village in Pittsfield, Massachusetts, from May through October 2005. The collection has been featured on cable television, one program earning an honorable mention Communicator Award, and has been the subject of several newspaper and magazine articles.

ABOUT THE AUTHOR

A retired banking executive whose lifelong love for the Stars and Stripes parallels his strong interest in politics and United States history, J. Richard Pierce has been collecting American parade flags since 1991.

He holds a degree in political science from Rutgers University and is a recipient of the prestigious Loyal Sons Award for extraordinary service to his alma mater. He served in the U.S. Army and Army Reserves.

Pierce is a guest lecturer and luncheon speaker for business associations, historical societies, and service organizations. He and his wife, Barbara, live in New Jersey; they have two children and four grandchildren.

Photo by: Mary Ellen Morris

ACKNOWLEDGMENTS

The author wishes to express his grateful appreciation and sincere personal thanks to the following individuals for their guidance and collective efforts in making this book a reality; and to others for their assistance in helping to assemble one of the finest parade flag collections in the country.

My wife, Barbara, for the inspiration, support, and encouragement she has given me to write this book and to take on numerous other projects; for sharing my love of the Stars and Stripes and for her suggestions and editing skills in proofreading the final draft.

Dr. Jeffrey Kenneth Kohn, for his longtime friendship and for finding so many rare and unusual flags for me over the years; for his invaluable assistance and knowledge in refining the content of this book.

Ron Toelke and Barbara Kempler-Toelke, of Toelke Associates, for their creativity and design expertise and for their guidance throughout the entire publication process.

Jeff Bridgman, of Jeff R. Bridgman American Antiques, for his friendship and for being one of the major sources from which I have acquired a large number of great flags.

Michael Fredericks, for the outstanding photographs used throughout this book.

Sarah Novak, for a superb job of editing the book's content and proofreading the final manuscript.

And special thanks to the many persons who had the foresight to record for posterity the stories and memorable moments revealed within the pages of this book.

SELECTED BIBLIOGRAPHY

Corcoran, Michael. *For Which it Stands: An Anecdotal History of the American Flag.* New York: Simon & Schuster, 2002.

Cornog, Evan, and Richard Whelan. *Hats in the Ring: An Illustrated History of American Presidential Campaigns.* New York: Random House, 2000.

Furlong, William Rea, and Byron McCandless. *So Proudly We Hail: The History of the United States Flag.* Washington, D.C.: Smithsonian Institution Press, 1981.

Guenter, Scot M. *The American Flag, 1777–1924: Cultural Shifts from Creation to Codification.* Madison, New Jersey: Fairleigh Dickinson University Press, 1990.

Mastai, Boleslaw, and Marie-Louise d'Otrange Mastai. *The Stars and the Stripes: The American Flag as Art and as History from the Birth of the Republic to the Present.* New York: Knopf, 1973.

GLOSSARY OF FLAG TERMS

appliqué: A piece of material sewn or stitched to the surface of another.

battle honor: The name of the battle or engagement in which a military unit fought.

canton: The upper left corner of the flag adjacent to the staff; also referred to as the union.

ensign: A national flag flown from the stern (back) of a naval vessel.

field: The background area of a flag on which the stars and stripes are placed.

finial: A decorative ornament on the top of a staff, usually an arrow, ball, or eagle.

fly: The free-flying vertical edge of the flag farthest from the staff; also referred to as the length of the flag.

fringe: A decorative edging of hanging threads or braiding attached to the three edges of the flag away from the staff.

"Great Star" pattern: A configuration of stars forming a large star.

guidon: A small military flag, usually in the form of a swallowtail, used in battle to identify the unit and to direct the movement of troops, especially cavalry.

halo: An outlined or framed star.

hoist: The vertical edge of a flag nearest the staff; also referred to as the width of the flag.

inscription: Words, names, and other notations handwritten on the face of a flag that record a specific moment in time or describe an event or purpose for which a flag was used.

medallion: A wreath or circle of stars.

obverse: The face of the flag when the hoist edge is at the viewer's left.

overprint: Words, letters, and symbols printed or stamped on the face of a flag that commemorate an event, advertise a product, or promote a political candidate.

reunion: A gathering of Civil War veterans to renew friendships and camaraderie and to discuss matters of importance to the veterans' movement; also referred to as an encampment.

reverse: The face of the flag when the hoist edge is at the viewer's right.

selvage: The edge or margin of fabric that has been tightly woven to prevent fraying or unraveling.

sleeve: A doubled-over piece of cloth attached to reinforce the hoist and through which the staff is placed.

staff: A pole on which a flag is attached for flying; during the Civil War, referred to as a pike by infantry units and a lance by cavalry units.

swallowtail: A flag with a V-shaped fly that enables it to remain straight in the wind so it can be readily identified from a distance.

"Third Maryland" pattern: An oval of twelve stars surrounding a central star; the design is believed to have been used originally by a regiment of Maryland soldiers at the battle of Cowpens during the Revolutionary War.

vexillology: The study of flags, their history, and symbolism.

CHRONOLOGY OF THE AMERICAN FLAG

This chronology traces the evolution of the Stars and Stripes from its original thirteen stars in 1777 to the present day fifty-star flag. Each state is listed in the order in which it was admitted to the union. Since 1818, a star for each new state is added to the official flag on July 4 following the year of statehood. To date, there have been twenty-seven official flags of the United States, with the forty-eight-star flag having been in existence for the longest period of time. The current flag, commemorating the fiftieth state, Hawaii, will soon become the longest-lived in our nation's history.

Stars	Flag Date	State	Statehood Date	Stars	Flag Date	State	Statehood Date
		Delaware	December 7, 1787	26	July 4, 1837	Michigan	January 26, 1837
		Pennsylvania	December 12, 1787	27	July 4, 1845	Florida	March 3, 1845
		New Jersey	December 18, 1787	28	July 4, 1846	Texas	December 29, 1845
		Georgia	January 2, 1788	29	July 4, 1847	Iowa	December 28, 1846
		Connecticut	January 9, 1788	30	July 4, 1848	Wisconsin	May 29, 1848
		Massachusetts	February 6, 1788	31	July 4, 1851	California	September 9, 1850
		Maryland	April 28, 1788	32	July 4, 1858	Minnesota	May 11, 1858
		South Carolina	May 23, 1788	33	July 4, 1859	Oregon	February 14, 1859
		New Hampshire	June 21, 1788	34	July 4, 1861	Kansas	January 29, 1861
		Virginia	June 25, 1788	35	July 4, 1863	West Virginia	June 20, 1863
		New York	July 26, 1788	36	July 4, 1865	Nevada	October 31, 1864
		North Carolina	November 21, 1789	37	July 4, 1867	Nebraska	March 1, 1867
13	June 14, 1777	Rhode Island	May 29, 1790	38	July 4, 1877	Colorado	August 1, 1876
14		Vermont	March 4, 1791	39		North Dakota	November 2, 1889
15	May 1, 1795	Kentucky	June 1, 1792	40		South Dakota	November 2, 1889
16		Tennessee	June 1, 1796	41		Montana	November 8, 1889
17		Ohio	February 19, 1803	42		Washington	November 11, 1889
18		Louisiana	April 30, 1812	43	July 4, 1890	Idaho	July 3, 1890
19		Indiana	December 11, 1816	44	July 4, 1891	Wyoming	July 10, 1890
20	April 13, 1818	Mississippi	December 10, 1817	45	July 4, 1896	Utah	January 4, 1896
21	July 4, 1819	Illinois	December 3, 1818	46	July 4, 1908	Oklahoma	November 16, 1907
22		Alabama	December 14, 1819	47		New Mexico	January 6, 1912
23	July 4, 1820	Maine	March 15, 1820	48	July 4, 1912	Arizona	February 14, 1912
24	July 4, 1822	Missouri	August 10, 1821	49	July 4, 1959	Alaska	January 3, 1959
25	July 4, 1836	Arkansas	June 15, 1836	50	July 4, 1960	Hawaii	August 21, 1959